ARCHITECTURE AND ITS MODELS
IN SOUTH-EAST ASIA

To
Henri Chambert-Loir
Bruno Dagens
John Miksic

ARCHITECTURE AND ITS MODELS IN SOUTH-EAST ASIA

Jacques Dumarçay

Translated and edited by
Michael Smithies

Orchid Press

Jacques Dumarçay
Translated and edited by Michael Smithies
ARCHITECTURE AND ITS MODELS IN SOUTH-EAST ASIA

First published: as *L'architecture et ses modèles en Asie du sud-est*,
                        Paris, Oriens, 1998
First published in this edition: 2003

ORCHID PRESS
P.O. Box 19,
Yuttitham Post Office,
Bangkok 10907, Thailand
www.orchidbooks.com

© Orchid Press 2003

Cover illustration: The Temple of Bantay Srei, Angkor, Cambodia. Photograph by Craig Raksin. © Craig Raskin 2002

ISBN-10: 974-524-027-3
ISBN-13: 978-974-524-027-8

CONTENTS

LIST OF FIGURES

All drawings are by the author, except where stated.

ACKNOWLEDGEMENTS

I should like to thank all those who have helped me, my wife and my daughter Anne Garro, my colleagues at the Ecole Française d'Extrême Orient (EFEO), including Pascale Royère, and the publisher of the first French language edition, Oriens. It goes without saying that any errors and questionable hypotheses are mine.

INTRODUCTION

In the present work, I would like to describe how, by the simple application of a model, the master builders of South-East Asia desired to create order in the universe, and then to dramatize this action, showing its development over time.[1]

This presentation is in large part based on my architectural studies,[2] and those who have read them will find some repetition here. I request their indulgence, having preferred to repeat myself rather than refer to earlier works. I have tried to present an overview of architecture in South-East Asia (chiefly of Cambodia and Java) from the point of view of its conception and the use to which architectural models were put.

When a founder orders the construction of a building (and is the master of the undertaking), with the economic wherewithal to undertake the construction of a relatively modest structure, he refers to models existing in the collective memory of the group of persons to which he belongs. This is the case, even today, with numerous individual houses in the Indonesian archipelago. On the contrary, if the proposed undertaking is to take on a certain volume, the founder will ensure the collaboration of a master builder[3] who is reputed to know the models which correspond to the implementation of the project. Initially the master builder faithfully follows the model, no matter what the conditions; this is the case with certain Batak houses in Sumatra. However, the peculiarities of the site or an evolution in materials used (as that caused by the disappearance of large boles in Javanese forests) have often required an adaptation of the forms in the collective intelligence of the group confronted with these difficulties.

The study of animal behaviour demonstrates a collective intelligence when faced with similar problems. One of the best examples, simplifying matters in the extreme, is that of builder wasps, also known as mud daubers.[4] These

---

1 This follows on my Babel Ruiné, Paris, Oriens, 1996, in which I tried to demonstrate the devices of the master builders on the worksite, as with the use of perspective effects, to make a structure appear bigger than it is in reality.

2 Almost all published in the collection of the Mémoires archéologiques of the Ecole Française d'Extrême Orient (EFEO).

3 Epigraphs never mention the master builder, whereas the person ordering a temple is always indicated. However, an old inscription of the sixth-seventh century discovered at Phnom Ba The (today in Vietnam) notes 'For this God this large, durable, well-endowed brick chapel, though constructed in six months, is the work of the honourable Kuma Rembha and not that of any other person.' (Translation taken from G. Coedès, Etudes cambodgiennes, XXXI, 'A propos du Tchen-la d'eau' *Bulletin de l'Ecole Française d'Extrême Orient (BEFEO)* XXXV. This is an exceptional and perhaps unique case of a master builder jealous of his reputation.

4 Studied by E. Bonabeau. See E. Bonabeau and G. Theraulaz, coordinators, *Intelligence collective*, Paris, Hermes, 1994.

wasps have in the collective memory of their species the form of their nest and the way of building it, but it sometimes happens that one of the insects comes up against a difficulty which is not found in this memory. For example, if the topography of the place where the nest will be placed requires a variation in the height of a layer (the nest of these wasps is composed of layers, normally regular, of small pellets of mud), this is calculated and a pellet of mud, formed in the required size, is placed in position in such a way that the nest remains regular, in appearance, conforming to the model. Each wasp reacts, when faced with a similar problem, in the same manner.

During the final stage of this evolution of architectural approaches, the master builder frees himself of all the constraints of the models and of the collective intelligence, and has become capable of anticipating the appearance of the completed work, independently of any acquired architectural knowledge.

The creation of a model is a result of circumstances relating to acquired techniques at any given moment and of the functional purpose of the structure. Sometimes another factor is a regional expression or preference. Thus the oblong plan was probably preferred by the master builders of Funan at the beginning because it was easy to cover with wooden beamwork; but later, when buildings were roofed with brick corbelling, the oblong plan was still retained, even though it was poorly adapted to the architectural form; such is the difficulty of abandoning an established model.

Most often, the model appears to us already conceived as a viable ensemble, though one can trace the development of a structure like the Khmer baray or reservoir (see Chapter II). Under the pressure of agricultural techniques and climatic conditions, the model conceived for use on the slopes of a hill or a mountainous plateau was transposed and adapted for use in the plains. In spite of all the problems this caused, the model was reproduced over three hundred years, with only the interventions of the collective intelligence to adapt it to changed topographical conditions. The model was not completely fixed in form, and evolved under pressure from technical progress and also under the influence of perspective. The built structure produces a geometrical environment which favours the development of perspective, an unforeseen world. When it was realized that a structure could only be seen on a vanishing scale and that, as a consequence, the elements of the false storeys of the towers of Khmer shrines were not visible from the foot of the tower, these elements were no longer placed in position, though the principles of construction remained the same, namely a main building topped by false storeys. The structure is the same in its composition, only the invisible parts are not provided but remain in the memory of the spectator. These transformations, applied by the collective intelligence of groups of individuals constituted, in spite of everything, new forms which were not always well understood, and sometimes the elements of the early model reappear (see Chapters I and III).

Architecture also often expresses a political will. Great enterprises can be sometimes a kind of reassertion of the authority of a ruler over his subjects, and, of course, this is independent of any architectural evolution. This was the case at the beginning of the ninth century in the area where Buddhism and

Hinduism confronted each other in central Java, but it can also be an expression of autocratic will, as, for example, at the end of the twelfth century, when Jayavarman VII constructed all over his kingdom bridges of the same design, because he had changed the policy relating to water (see Chapter II). This enormous works programme, even if it made use of previous structures, contributed to the economic exhaustion of the country. It also had another consequence, that of dispersing authority and so weakening political power. It was also the period when architecture became dramatic, as recently built structures were destroyed shortly after they were completed, as at the Bapuon.

One moves from the use of models to a project making use of new forms, particular to the master builder who has seen their architectural possibilities (Chapter V). This appeared progressively in Cambodia from the beginning of the eleventh century and more decisively in Java during the fourteenth century. This was a complete break with the past; the master builder ceased to be one who merely applied formulae and used the collective memory, and became a creator of new volumes. This is particularly apparent at Angkor with the construction of Angkor Wat, or in Java with the temples of Jabung or Pari. From the moment when the architect anticipates the result of his creation, where he is master of the perspective vision of the building he is going to construct, he is going to seek to control the viewpoint of the spectator looking at his structure. This is the art of the architect of Angkor Wat, who knew how to arrange the different lines of sight so that they changed for the visitor as he progresses through the building. In this way one can imagine the temple as an enlarged projection which appears as expected, only when viewed from a particular point, as with someone looking at a curved distorting mirror.

When oriental architectural models became the vogue in Europe or, on the contrary, when certain western monuments were imposed on Asia, the different human groups used forms of the collective memory to adjust these imposed models to their advantage. For example, from the seventeenth to the nineteenth centuries, from England to Japan, the form of the Chinese pagoda was used with greater or lesser success: in England and France out of a taste for the oriental, in India to celebrate a battle, and in Japan for religious reasons. At that period, in those places, at Kew near London (fig.1), at Chanteloup close to the banks of the Loire (fig.2), at Manora near Pondicherry (fig.3), or at Aizu Wakamatu in Japan (fig.4), the master builders knew how to anticipate the completed structure but, with these four examples, one can readily find the characteristics of the original form. This is indeed the desired objective, but in each case the master builder was able to express his own talent and his own architectural formation. But it is not so obvious: if William Chambers was directly inspired by drawings of Chinese buildings, it is not the case of Camus de Mézière, the architect of Chanteloup, who was not inspired by a Chinese building but by the Kew pagoda itself; the process is similar for the pagoda at Manora where the master builder imitated Chambers. The most worrying building is the Japanese pagoda, where the interior of the tower is filled with a double stairway of western inspiration (probably that of the Château de Chambord, through an English treatise of the eighteenth century in which

1. *The Kew pagoda, near London, after a drawing by William Chambers published c.1720.*

2. Sketch of the Chanteloup pagoda, 1775-1778, near Amboise, France.

*3. Sketch of the Manora pagoda, near Pondicherry, India,
built to celebrate the battle of Waterloo.*

4. The pagoda of Aizu Wakamantu, Japan, built in 1796,
after the sketch of Kobayashi Bunji.

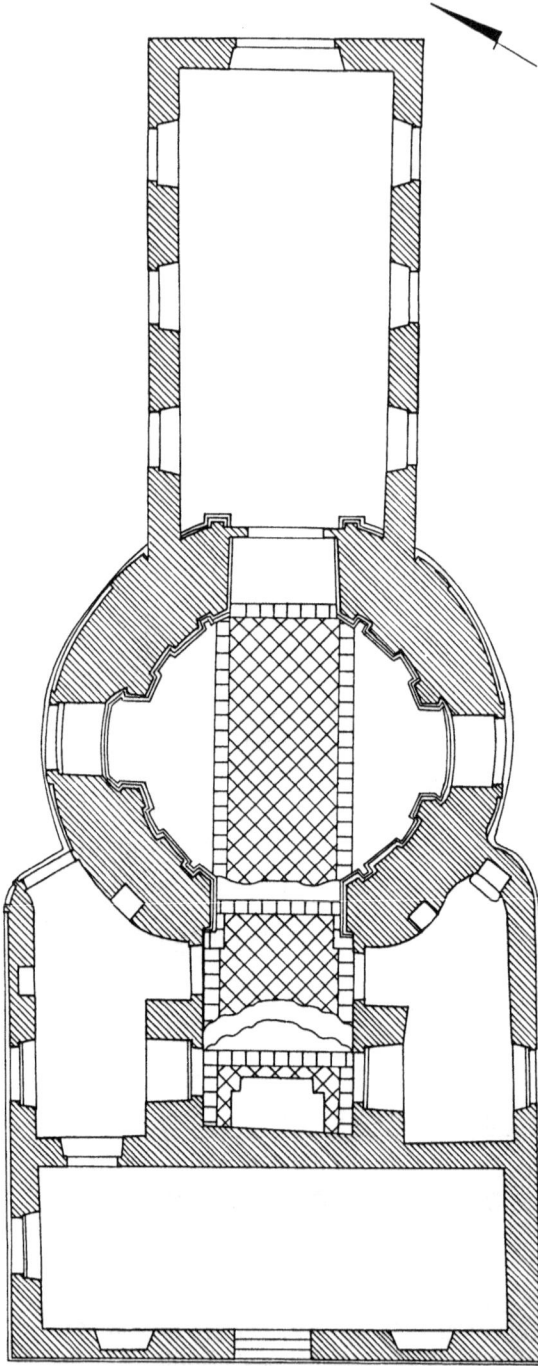

5. *Plan of the Nosa Chaldera church at Nanouar, Goa, India.*

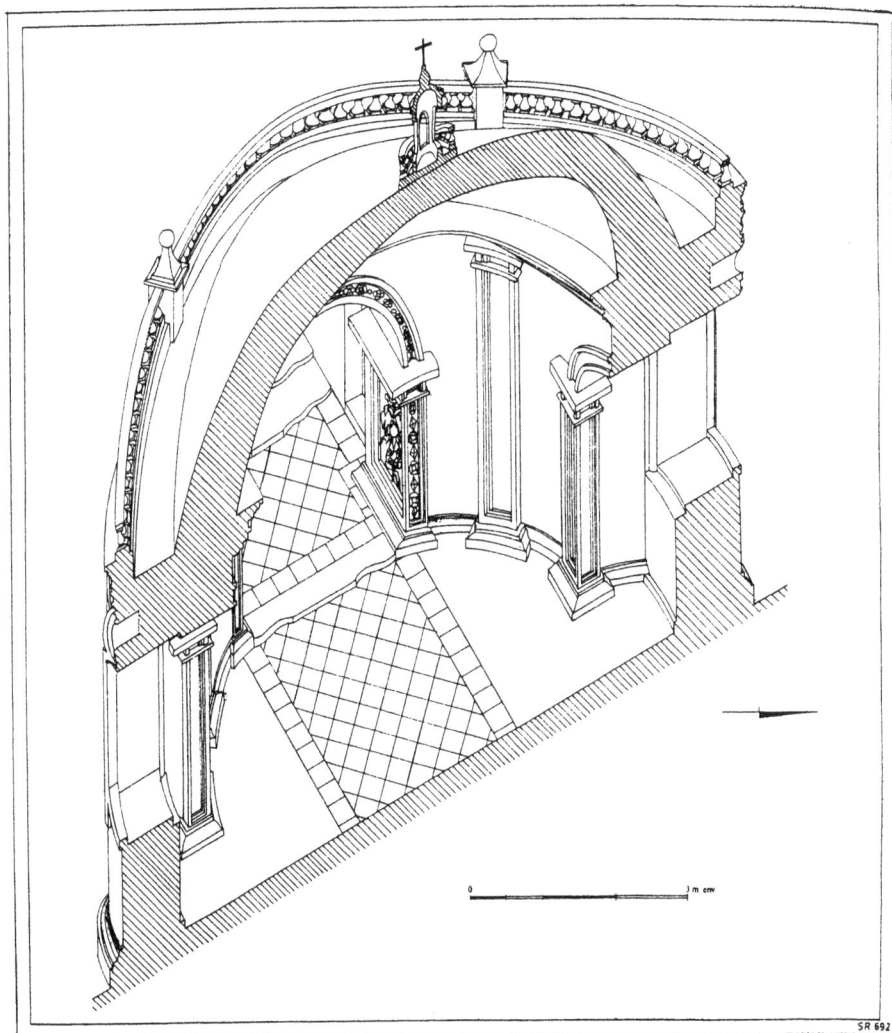

6. Axonometric drawing of the choir of Nosa Chaldera in Fig. 5.

a copy of a design of this nature is found), which was inserted, with some success, in a Chinese envelope, and created a case of architecture feeding on itself (see Chapter VI).

Missionaries in India built numerous churches in Goa (figs 5 and 6) or in the south in Pondicherry (fig.7) inspired by contemporary European models but creating new forms which were perhaps only blunders and were turned into points of reference; architecture fed on its own mistaken ideas and created a style. This can also be seen in Java, in some mosques in Jakarta for which the master builder most probably used an architectural treatise of the sixteenth century, that of Serlio, and reproduced his proportions for the Tuscan orders based on the size of columns, the amount of decoration, and so on. This example was subsequently spread throughout the island, in particular at Pasuruan, and the early fumblings were repeated ad infinitum. It can be seen that even when the model has lost its prestige it remains influential as long as the master builder does not have sufficient self-assurance. Such self-assurance only developed at the end of the nineteenth or even the beginning of the twentieth centuries.

When Le Corbusier[5] went to work in India, he was able to observe that Indian architects faced serious problems on their worksites, given the very uneven quality of the different trades employed in the construction of a building. He decided to eliminate as many small ones as possible and to keep but one, the makers of concrete, a single trade; this had considerable influence in India and transformed urban architecture, even influencing rural dwellings. The desire of Le Corbusier, favouring the use of concrete, profoundly influenced structures built without an architect, giving them their disordered modernity.

---

[5] Le Corbusier had for long desired a limit to sub-contracting and he wrote *Un seul corps de métier* in 1925.

7. *Sketch of the façade of the cathedral at Pondicherry, India.*

8. A palace of the chosen at Angkor Wat, south gallery, east wing, showing heavens and hells.

I

THE USE OF MODELS

The model was a necessity to facilitate the economic and symbolic evaluation of the completed structure. Models and treatises were a kind of guarantee that the completed building would please not only men but also the gods, if the structure were a temple. In this case the construction was often the dwelling of the god which had to be magnificent, located on Mount Meru, but a real mountain could not be built. Sometimes a natural site was used whose shape (a central peak with four outlying abutments) evoked the mythical mountain, as for example with Mount Penangunan in Java. Recourse to a model was indispensable to guarantee that the structure was aesthetically beautiful, and the treatises had no other purpose than to ensure this.

The architecture of the sacred mountain had to be of a higher order of beauty than in nature, though its aesthetics were neither readily transposable nor even correctly perceived. The silhouette of Mount Penangungan is reproduced on the reliefs at Candi Jawi, but it is not certain that the beauty of its form was appreciated, except in that it recalled the traditional descriptions. The mythical images had to be translated into architectural forms, with models which were known, and to introduce a spatial geometry. As noted in the introduction, this caused unforeseen viewpoints because of perspective. It was the perspective effects which caused an evolution in architectural forms, which, nevertheless, remained in conformity with the original structure. Thus the five peaks of the mythical mountain were transformed in Cambodia into five sanctuary towers conforming to models already established. To suggest the five peaks, the central shrine was simply enlarged, to demonstrate its pre-eminence. When the representation of the dwelling of a god was shown as a flying palace in architectural volume, it was given winged animals to carry it (fig. 8). Thus in the reliefs depicting the heavens and hells at Angkor Wat, the chosen reside in palaces borne by flying creatures because they are close to the gods.

The civilizations of South-East Asia first came into contact with Indian architecture through wooden buildings, and wood was the material used in the early shrines in the region. We know this thanks to reliefs we have showing these buildings, notably those at Borobudur (fig. 9).

The art said to be of Funan in Cambodia preferred rectangular forms deriving from a wooden model which is easy to cover with beamwork. The oblong plan is found at Sambor Prei Kuk, Wat Phu, and Prasat Andet (figs 10 and 11), as well as at Angkor, in Phimeanakas, which is also built on a rectangular plan. Some traces of buildings now in the courtyard of the royal palace also have an oblong plan, as do the two side shrines of the Kutisvara temple.[1] It is probable

---

[1]   The Kutisvara temple is discussed in H. Marchal's 'Kutiçvara', *BEFEO* XXXVII, pp.333-56.

9. *A building shown in panel 13 on the south side of the third gallery at Borobudur, Java.*

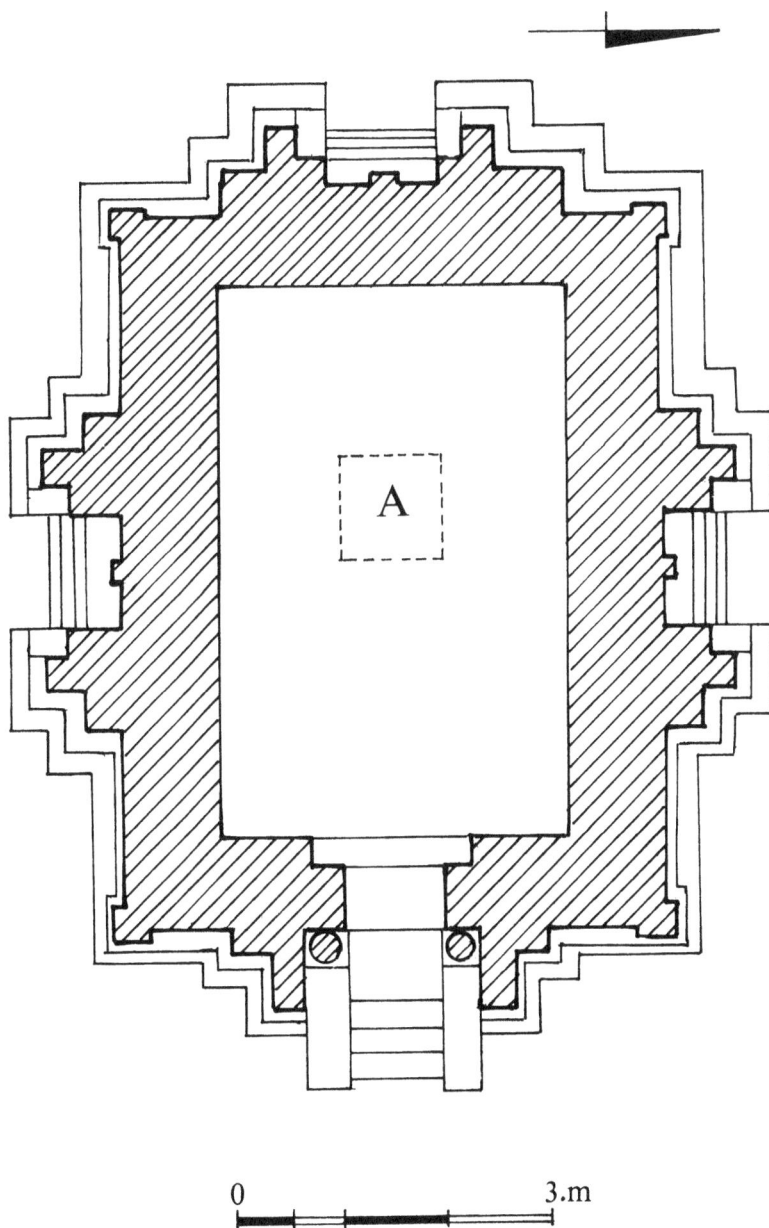

10. Plan of Praset Andet, Angkor, after a drawing by H. Parmentier.

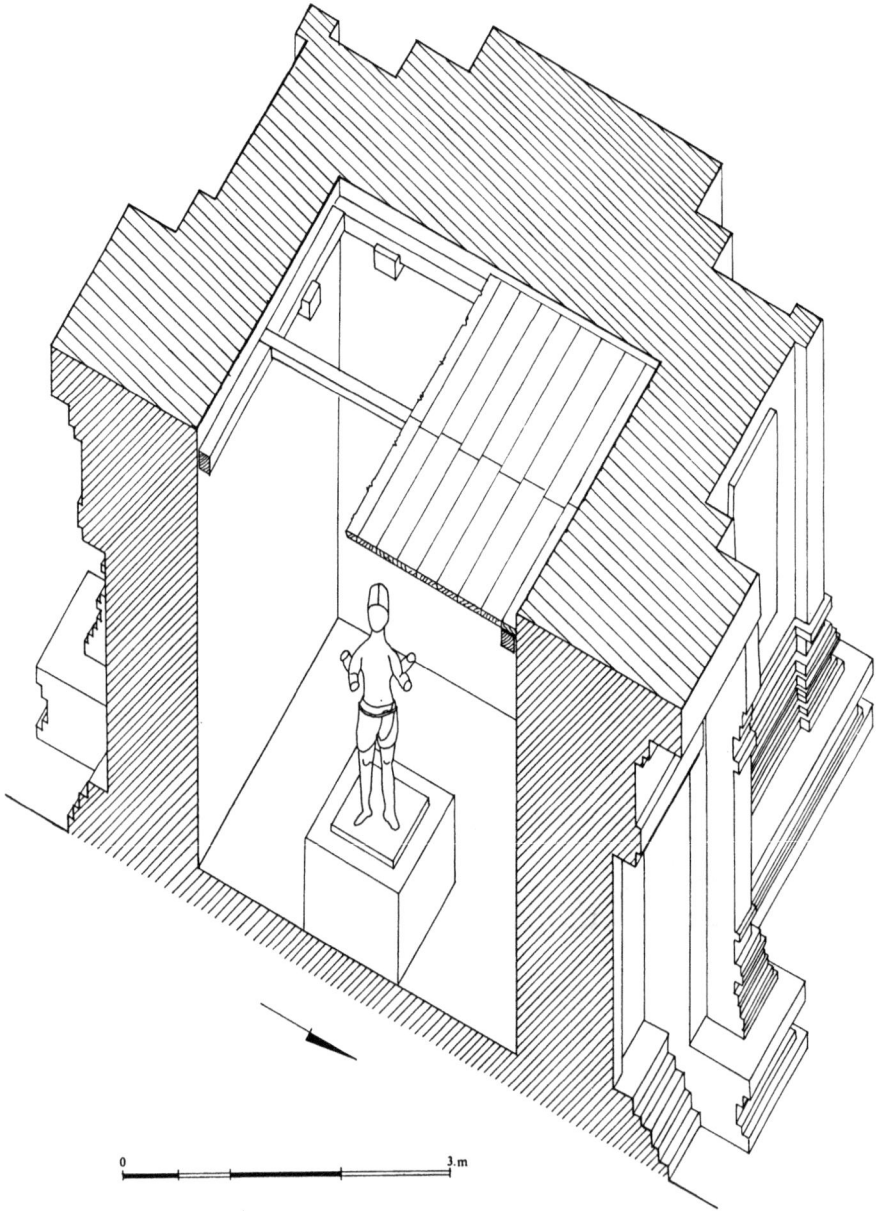

11. *Axonometric perspective of the interior of the cella of Prasat Andet.*

that when Yasovarman established himself at the site of Angkor, he found a small Funan settlement (fig.12) centring on Phimeanakas (fig. 13). The town attributed to Yasovarman has such important dimensions[2] that they seem improbable; moreover the incomplete double enclosure seems to us to postdate the construction of the Western Baray, that is from the eleventh century; the external wall stops at the southern bank of the baray, and the internal wall is found at the south-east corner of the huge reservoir which was built in three stages. When Yasovarman and his successors came from Roluos, and built at Angkor, they brought not only new techniques for irrigation, which must have been difficult to assimilate successfully (the construction of such a huge undertaking at the Eastern Baray must indeed have been a tough experience for the early inhabitants), but also architectural models where the square plan was predominant. Structures with an oblong plan were abandoned for a long time, except for chambers with a roof-covering of beamwork in the tenth and eleventh centuries (at Pre Rup and Ta Keo, for example), and some other adjacent buildings.

Models evolve according to technical progress. This can be seen in Sambor Prei Kuk where several octagonal temples were constructed on the same model but each differed slightly in construction details,[3] in particular in relation to the doorways (figs 14,15, and 16). It can be seen from this example that, even when the model is closely followed, construction techniques caused the architecture to evolve; in this precise case the transformation of the door casings somewhat lightened the structure.

Construction techniques can have much greater influence. In Java, under the Sailendra dynasty, probably with Singhalese influence, the master builders adopted a construction technique which relies on the coefficient of the friction of stones. This consists of blocking the masonry courses by forcing into place a stone wedge; this pushes the courses towards the corners and ensures a better cohesion to the whole.

This was particularly noticeable in Cambodia when the qualities of sandstone were better appreciated, notably the nature of its grain, which could take advantage of friction, an essential element in constructions built without the use of mortar. The use of forcing wedges caused a considerable evolution in construction methods; in Cambodia they were first used in laterite, and in Java with adesite, but only in the vertical plane. With sandstone a real stereotomy would be employed, using forcing wedges in the horizontal plane as

---

The article is illustrated by a plan of the complex (pl.LV). Marchal dates the central shrine, which is square in plan, to the end of the ninth century, and the side chapels to the tenth century.

[2] V. Goloubew, 'Le Phom Bakheng et la ville de Yaçovarman,' *BEFEO* XXXIII, 1933.

[3] In the south group at Sambor Prei Kuk, there are two octagonal towers, S7 and S11, probably built at the same time, but differing considerably in their length, though they have the same plan (see H. Parmentier, *L'art khmer primitif*, Paris, EFEO 1927, pl.XV); it is only in the north group that the plan changes a little, where the octagon is irregular (see fig. 15).

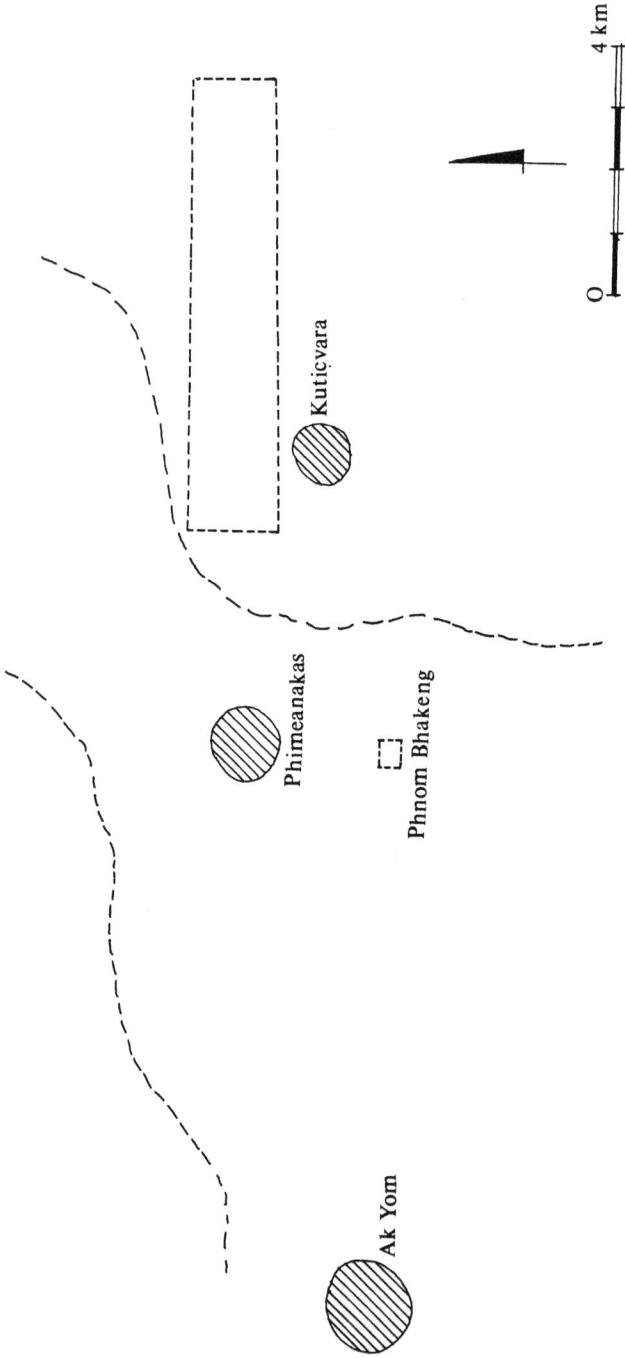

12. Occupation of the site of Angkor before the laying out of the Eastern Baray.

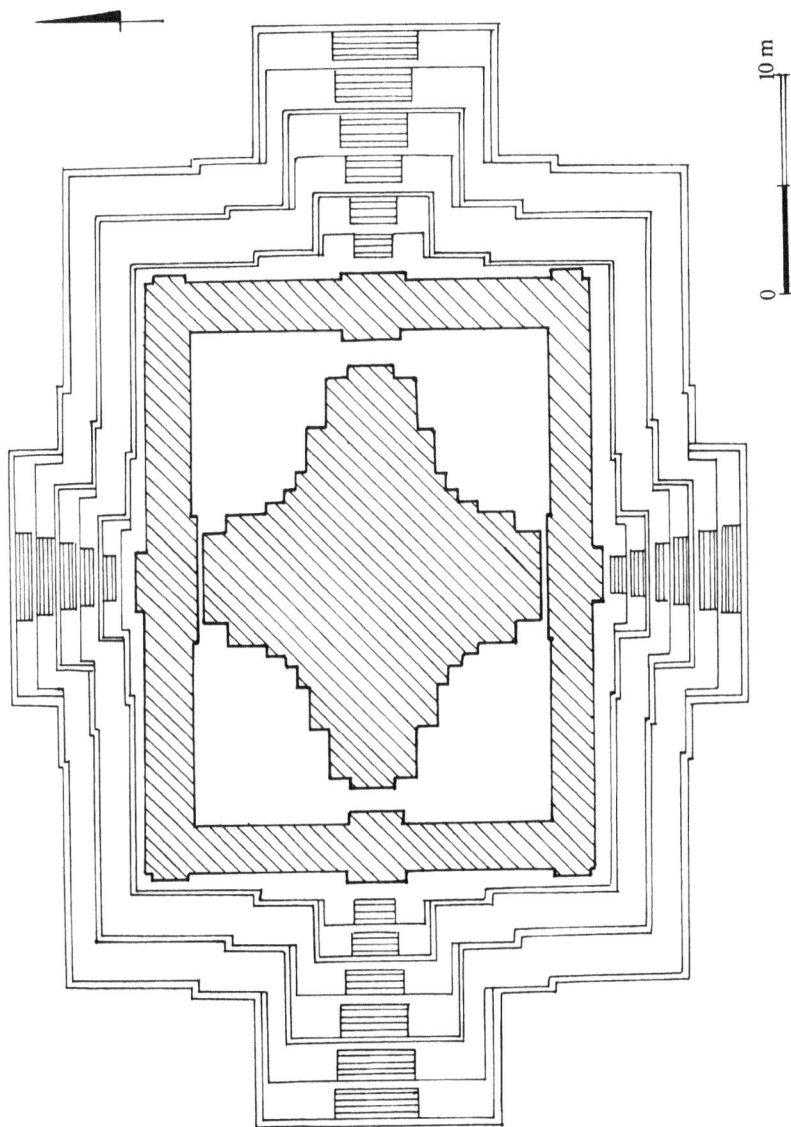

13. Plan of Phimeanakas, Angkor; the cross-hatched parts indicate the location of elements added after the disappearance of wooden structures.

10 m

0

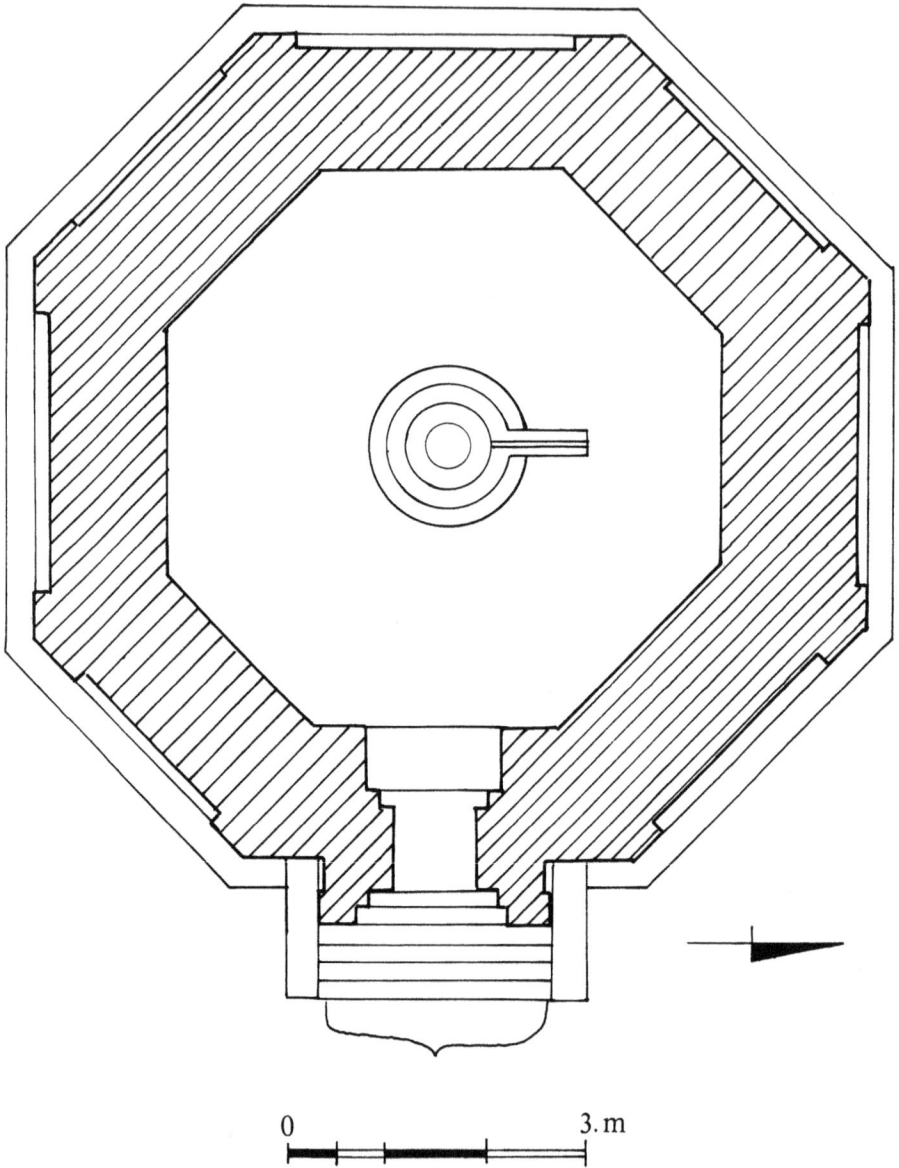

0   3. m

14. Tower S7, south group, Sambor Prei Kuk, Cambodia.

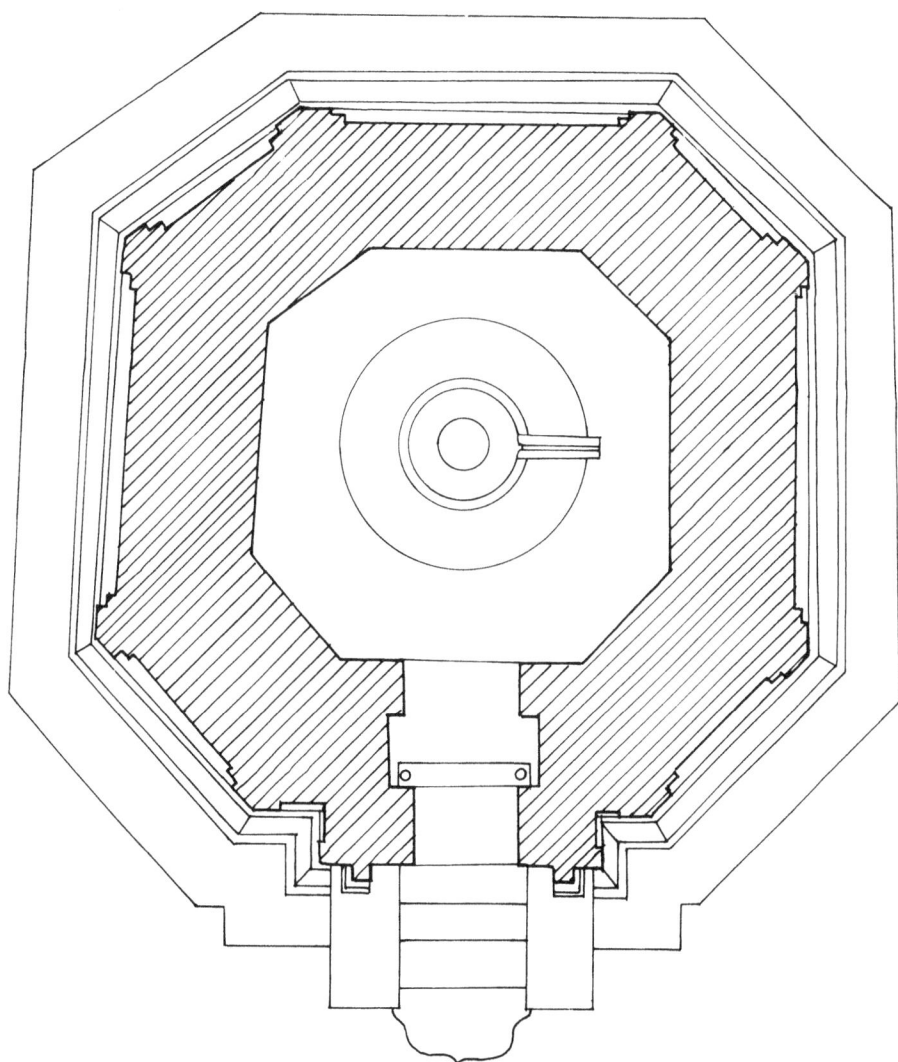

15. *Tower N7, north group, Sambor Prei Kuk.*

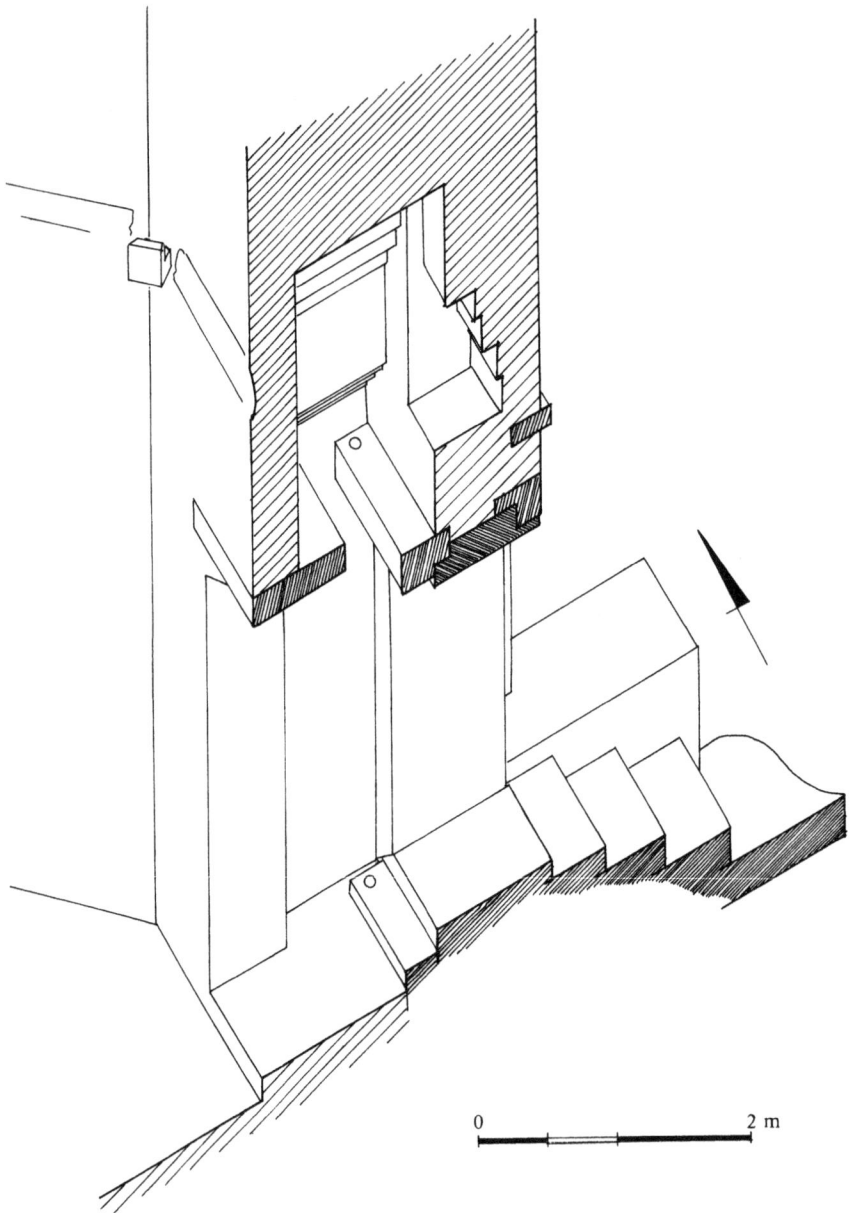

16. *Axonometric drawing of the door frames and their insertion in the masonry, tower N7, north group, Sambor Prei Kuk.*

well. Stones were cut at a distance from the work site, in a kind of stone-cut-ters hut. The cutting struck the imagination of the artists; among the tortures which the damned undergo, illustrated in the huge relief decorating the east gallery of the south façade at Angkor Wat, two tortures were envisaged by the artists, directly related to this technique (figs 17 and 18). In one, the damned are inserted under a mountain and are ground as were the bottoms of the stones, and in the other (marked by a small inscription translated by G. Coedès, 'the twin mountains'[4]), the damned are caught between two mountains and ground like the sides of the stones. This important technical advance was used early on in the huge shrine of the Bapuon, but the flowering of the technique is found in Angkor Wat. The method continued to be employed in the twelfth and thirteenth centuries; the cutting and the grinding of stones are shown in the reliefs found at the Bayon.[5]

This technical progress did not point the way to other possibilities to the master builders, and this is probably one of the reasons why they abandoned only very slowly the constraints of the models. The technique was indeed used sparingly in spite of the excellent results obtained in laterite at Phimeanakas. When the sandstone construction of Phnom Bakheng temple was begun, the wedges were really only used on the superstructures, in combination with tenons and mortices. The pyramid was constructed essentially by using angle brackets in the vertical plane, which was one of the techniques used in Boro-budur after the sixty-fifth course, with some forcing wedges only in the vertical plane (fig.19; this is one of the earliest appearances of this technique in the region, in the last years of the eighth century). For the period, it represented a considerable progress since the angle bracket retains the courses one above the other under pressure from the internal fill.[6]

The forms of the shrine of Phnom Bakheng are faithful to the model, and the general layout of the temple only differs from the model in relation to the work programme to the space it occupied (see Chapter V). If, as J. Filliozat claimed, Phnom Bakheng is a representation of the phases of the planet Ju-piter, the layout had to conform to this parameter, but each of the elements remains similar to traditional structures. Thus the model of the sanctuary-tower is found, in different contexts, at Prasat Kravan which is dedicated to Vishnu, and at Prasat Bei, with only three towers and so probably Shivaite. The work programme changed, but not the model. When the work programme became more complicated, as at Pre Rup or the Eastern Mebon, the differences are found in the laying out and the meaning given to the structure, but the struc-tures remain essentially the same.

In Java, about AD 790, a very important religious change took place in

---

[4] G. Coedès, *Les bas-reliefs d'Angkor Wat*, Mémoires archéologiques de l'EFEO II, Paris, 1923.

[5] On the reliefs of the second gallery between towers 30 and 31.

[6] This technical improvement was probably the result of a collapse on the north side of the monument during the construction works.

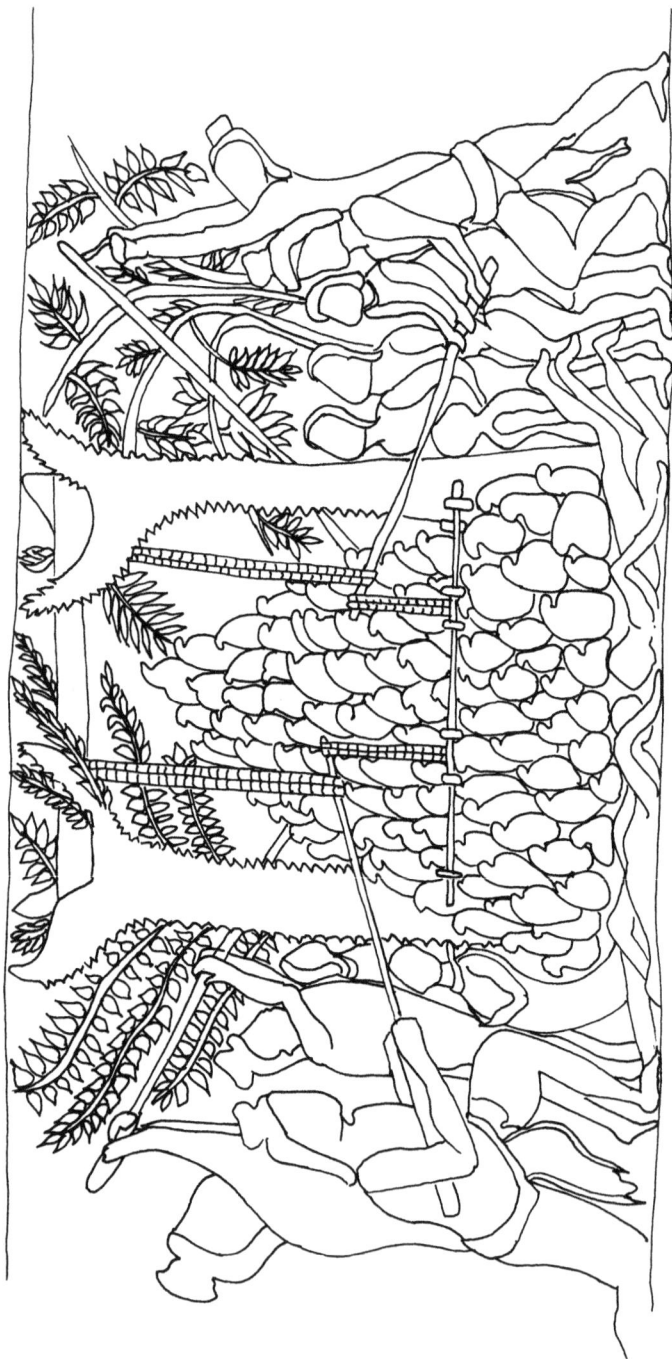

17. One of the tortures of the damned, the grinding, in the gallery of heavens and hells at Angkor Wat.

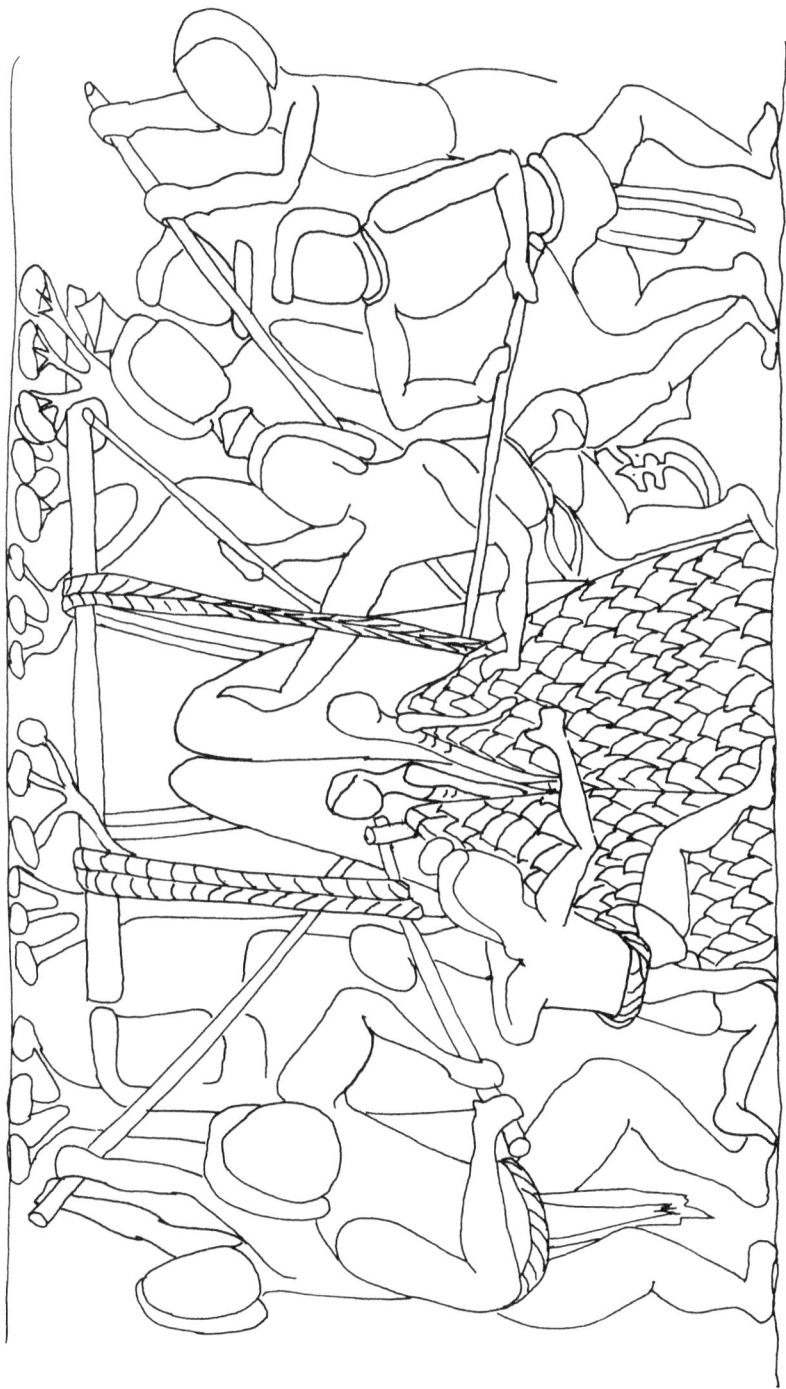

18. *The torture of the twin mountains, indicated as such by an inscription above the relief, in the gallery of heavens and hells at Angkor Wat.*

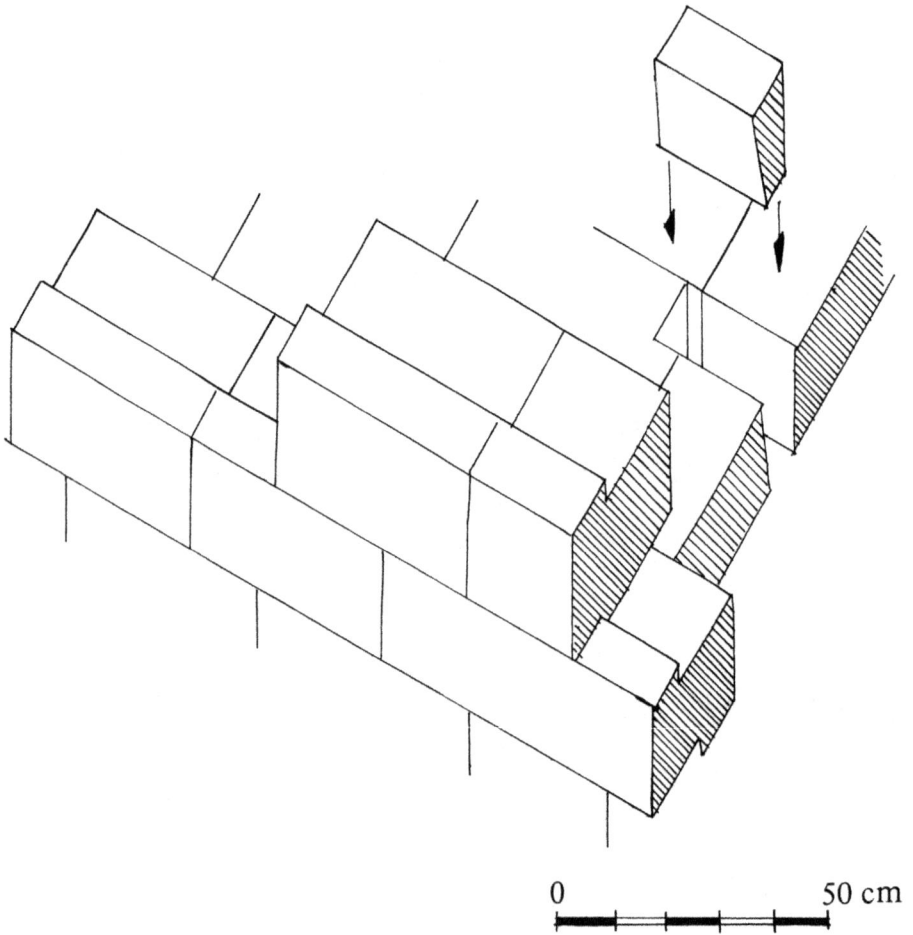

0   50 cm

19. The insertion of the masonry above the 65th layer at Borobudur, Java.

the centre of the island. From a form of Buddhism probably very close to that practised in Ceylon, there was a shift to the cult of the five Jina. The change in architecture was considerable. Candi Sewu and all its related buildings were modified, as was Candi Kalasan and numerous small temples built on the same model but with different layouts. Rather than constructing new temples, at the beginning at least the existing structures were changed, either out of a sense of urgency or simply for the sake of economy.[7] In spite of this the changes in religious practices sometimes involved major alterations, hardly less than the work required to build a new temple, as at Candi Kalasan, for example, where the temple was completely revamped. More often, though, a few alterations were sufficient, and did not make drastic changes to the temple; for the new rites the addition of doorways was required and this was begun, but never completed, on all the small temples surrounding Candi Sewu. On the central shrine, the changes were major and profoundly changed the building. Some-times the temple was not well adapted to the changes, as at Candi Lumbung, where the side cella of the central shrine were reduced to mere niches for statues of standing divinities. The master builder in charge of these works thought it sufficient here to insert a door opening to the exterior (which was probably not in conformity with the rites, as generally the doors opened inwards where they could be closed by the officiating dignitary inside the cella); this hardly changed the original temple and scarcely marked the novelty of the changes. At the time of this religious reform, several Hindu temples in the region were also transformed into Buddhist shrines by the addition of a doorway. Some-times this was done rather belatedly, as at Candi Gebang where the new rites were only just adopted at the beginning of the ninth century; not only was a doorway added here, but the boundary markers were put in position, which gives a chronological indication for the changes to the temple. On the Dieng plateau, other temples underwent this type of work programme; for example Candi Bima had its doorways completely changed and the addition there of an octagonal terrace is probably another indication of the shift to Buddhism (the addition of an octagonal element to the terminal decoration of Candi Kalasan was also part of its modifications). These few examples demonstrate how much the architectural model was independent of the meaning to be ascribed to it. However, once transformed (as with the addition of a doorway) the change was incorporated in the model and all the temples built after the reform include the doorways required for the new rites.

It can be seen how much the architectural models persisted in spite of all the religious and political changes; even when the master builder became capable of anticipating the form of the completed building, he continued for a long time to refer back to acquired structural knowledge. In spite of all the new features of the Bayon, in spite of the procedures the master builder employed which were different from those used in previous periods, the face-towers of

---

[7] The changes at Candi Sewu were studied in J. Dumarçay, *Candi Sewu et l'architecture bouddhique du centre du Java*, Paris, EFEO, 1981.

the Bayon are but the expression of the model of the ninth century shrine, on which monumental faces on four sides were placed at the height of the second false storey. In Java at the end of the tenth century, the model built at Dieng and Gedong Songo probably spread throughout east Java and even beyond, to Bali: on this island can be seen on a rock structure of the eleventh century transformations which were perhaps only due to the shift from a built structure to a carved structure, but the form of this structure became general in Java in the thirteenth century, sometimes with a completely different meaning, as the Balinese temples often had a funerary purpose. Thus at Badjang Ratu, on the probable site of the Majapahit capital, the model was perfectly copied, not for a temple but for a gateway. Even when the master builders truly anticipated the completed building, they did not always break with the model; at Candi Jabung, in spite of the novelty of its circular plan, the upper part of the door-frames reproduce the model of the thirteenth century.

The models were used with some liberty: the oblong shrines of the royal palace at Angkor (fig. 20)[8] have the same plan and are aligned on the same axis, but their dimensions vary, not very much but all the same in a significant way—the lengths of the four temples, from north to south, are respectively 9.23m, 9.26m, 9.25m, and 9.30m. The first three can be considered similar, but this is not so when the two end shrines are compared. The 7cm difference cannot be explained by the cut necessary for the redressed surface; its volume, though significant, did not reach 7cm. So it points either to carelessness in the laying out,[9] or an inability to obtain a desired value. This is still more evident in Java, at Candi Sewu, where the central shrine is surrounded by 244 chapels, all on the same plan, but with significant variations,[10] and it is possible that the initial laying-out was less than careful, but certain proportions had to be observed, in particular in the difference in the heights of the decorative panels. So whatever its orientation, the panel opposite a door was higher, and corresponds to a difference in motif. On each of the towers of the first row, the person in the centre of the panel opposite the door is upright, but on the side panels bends at the hips. This position no doubt in part explains the differences in the height of the panels, but they remain close to the model since the tracing of the figures is clearly posterior to the placing of the cornices. At a much later date, when the architectural treatises were codified, particularly in Bali, it was given out that side doors should be markedly lower than the main door. This has an ancient origin since these differences can be found in temples of

---

[8] These buildings were frequently remodelled, in particular, when their roofs were already ruined, they were adapted with a roofing supported by wooden beamwork itself supported by posts inserted in the base; their original plan can still be seen.

[9] The Khmers only had, for laying out, a very simple tool for overall alignment, the alidade; for small constructions they probably used an angle bracket which was not always very exact.

[10] P. Lordereau indicated all these variations in his study of the Javanese cubits in *Candi Sewu...* op.cit.

37

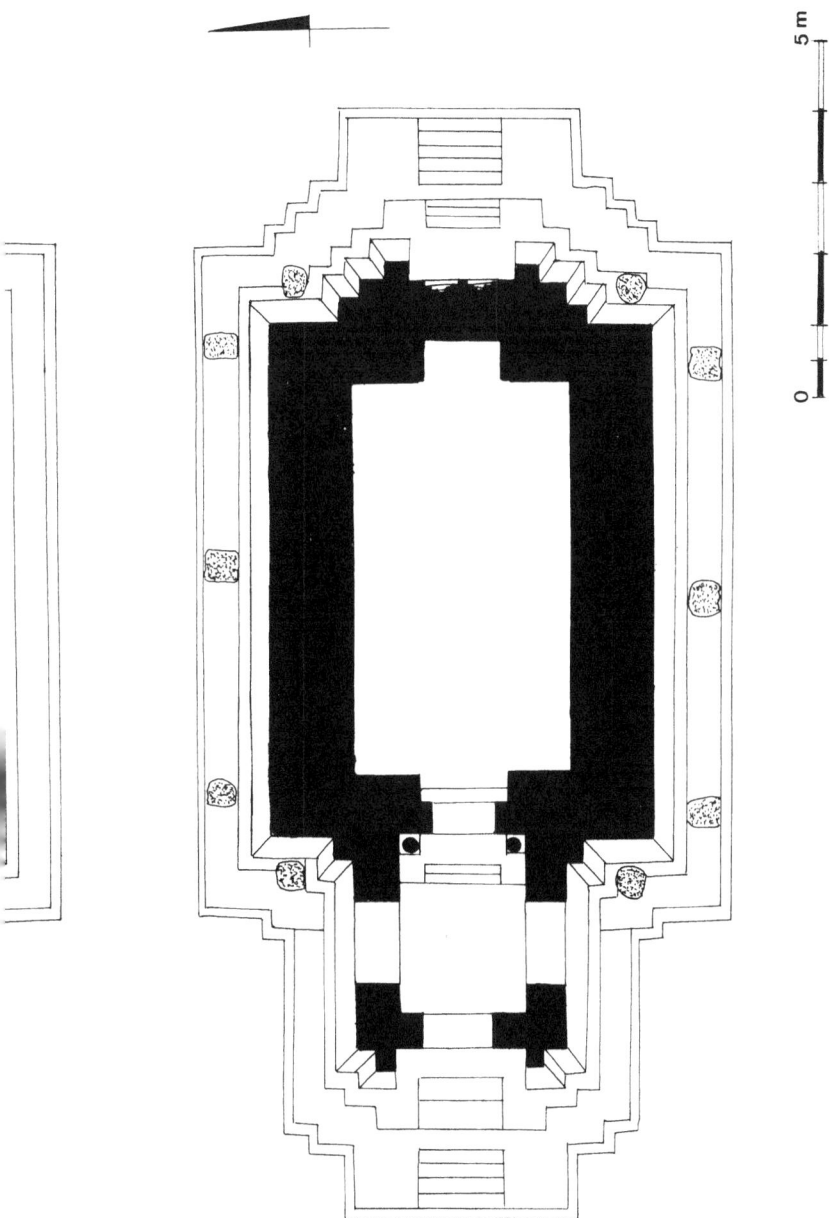

20. One of the long structures called 'stores' in the enclosure of the royal palace at Angkor, after a drawing of the EFEO.

the thirteenth century, at Candi Kidal, for example. As time passed, reference
to the model was reduced to very little. The temple of Singosari, which has a
cruciform plan, probably refers to the same model as Candi Sembodro on the
Dieng plateau, and though the volumes and decoration are indeed different,
the proportions of the plan are identical, not only for the main structure but
also for its foundation base.

The use of a pre-established form was generally applied to the decoration,
and architectural styles have been determined from this, sometimes independently of the history of the monuments. When the building has a complex
history, as is the case with Borobudur, the master builders successively tried to
obtain a unity through the decoration, even if the laying out of the structures
were different.

One of the most constant elements of Khmer architectural decoration is
the false lintel in front of the entrance doorway. The ornamentation of the
Khmer lintel consists mostly of garlands and decorative drops such as covered
the temple on feast days; in carving them in stone that day was to a certain
extent fixed in time. Temporary structures were built in front of the temple;
this tradition is maintained today and provisional structures in front of the
temple entrance are still erected, sometimes of great complexity. These will
have a lintel consisting of leaf scrolls held in position by brass rings (fig. 21;
letters A, B and C indicate the rings, and this element is found in fig. 22,
carved in stone). This group is placed on the trunks of two carved banana
trees. The Khmer sculptors translated this into stone, giving a longer life to
the ephemeral form (fig. 22). In the nineteenth century in Thailand, when
wooden temples were restored, the lintel too was made of wood, but remained
close to the model (fig. 23). In spite of all the variations in this detail, over
the centuries the original figuration of a vegetal form remains, the image of
an ephemeral moment. The same is true in Java: the head of the monster
over the doorways, in spite of all its transformations, remains in conformity
with the model. If the style of the decoration enables historians to date the
building, its general lines remain the same over several centuries (fig. 24a
shows the head seen in Candi Lumbung, dating to about AD 800, fig. 24b
the head at Candi Kidal, dating from the thirteenth century, and in fig. 64
can be seen the head found in Candi Jabung, from the fourteenth century).
The continuity of this decorative form remains striking.

The overall composition of the outline of a building corresponds to
hierarchies of different architectural elements, which are also models. Indian
architectural treatises give over much space to the description[11] of these outlines
and continued to be followed, even though architectural composition was freed;
thus at Angkor Wat, the hierarchies of the outlines continue to be observed
on a building which no longer conforms to the forms previously applied. The

---

[11] For example, in the *Mayamata*, the description of the successions of mouldings is discussed
in extenso. B. Dagens, *Mayamata, traité sanscrit d'architecture*, Pondicherry, Institut
Français d'Indologie, 1970.

21. Schema showing the positioning of the leaf scrolls for a provisional decoration in front of a Cambodian temple.

0   10 cm

22. Fragment of a lintel at the Eastern Mebon, Angkor,
after a drawing by the EFEO.

0   30 cm.env.

23. Wooden lintel at a temple doorway in Thailand.

24. Central decorative motifs of two Javanese temples:
(a) Candi Lumbung, (b) Candi Kidal.

model of the outline can be reduced as follows: the pre-eminence of the main building over all the other elements which it should dominate even if it results in some incoherence; for example, there is never any concordance in the order of the mouldings (fig. 25) when one moves from one part of the building to another. If the architect of Angkor Wat completely changed the architectural composition, he retained the earlier ornamental devices with a few corrections; to avoid the impression of the stairways being embedded in the structure, the plinth of their string walls is skewed instead of being horizontal (fig. 26a, and the dotted line b indicate the reconstituted visual level) which corrects this deformation.

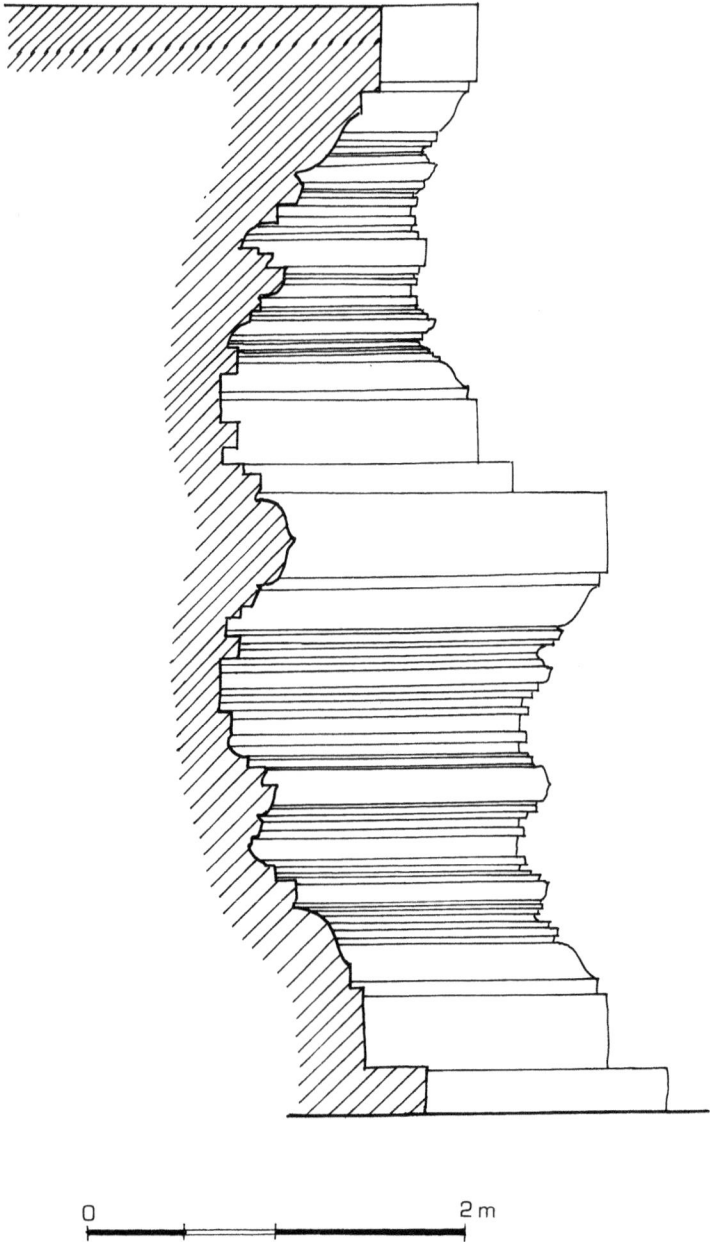

25. Cross-section of the outline of the third step of the foundation wall
on the terrace of the third level of Ta Keo at Angkor, and the elevation
of the outline of the string walls of the third flight of stairs.

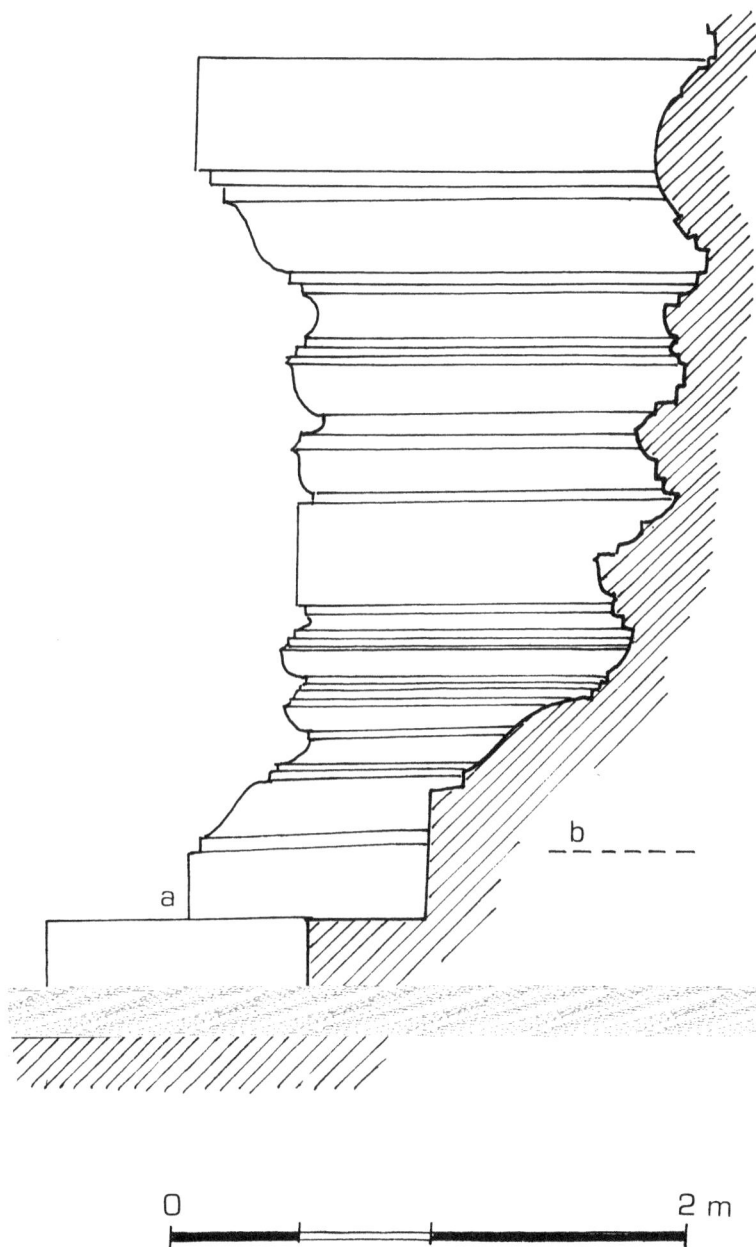

26. *Outline of the base of a projecting step on the base of the retaining wall
of the upper terrace at Angkor Wat: (a) the recess of the plinth,
(b) its visual correction.*

II

THE BARAY AND COLLECTIVE INTELLIGENCE

However simple an architectural project might be, a certain economic surplus is necessary for it to be built. This is particularly true of the old Khmer kingdom which was essentially an agricultural power. Consequently, improvements in agricultural production were expected to provide the necessary economic surplus. The chief Cambodian product was (and remains) rice, and the rains and floods decided whether a harvest were abundant or insufficient. The harvest also depended on the type of irrigation used, which in the region of Battambang and Siem Reap was just gravitational flow. The longest growing cycle for rice of the best quality, from seeding to harvesting, is seven to eight months; from the end of April the seed beds are prepared and sown at the beginning of May (when the dry season is more marked than usual, the seedlings sometimes have to be watered until the beginning of June). At the beginning of July the rice plants are taken from the seed beds and the planting out is begun; this is usually complete by the beginning of the heavier rains in August. From mid-September to the beginning of November the paddy fields are flooded (in some years the floods may last until the end of November), but generally the ears of rice can be seen in mid-November; from the end of this month until January, the rice is harvested, threshed, and the waste turned into fodder.

In addition to good quality rice, a quicker-growing rice with lower yields is also planted; the complete cycle only takes four months, or sometimes, in favourable years, only three months. Another kind known as 'subsidence rice' is also grown on the banks of the Tonle Sap, which is only harvested at the end of January.[1]

Because of this timetable it can be seen that the need for water starts in July and is most important from September to mid-November. If the rains are sufficient in this period, the naturally occurring floods ensure a good harvest, but if there is too much difference between the water available and that needed, the harvest runs the risk of being disastrous.[2] In this case only the

---

[1] Rice cultivation by gravity flow was studied in many official reports when a land register was to be established in order to collect a land tax. In a report on rice cultivation in Indochina of 1931 it was stated, in relation to the rice fields of the Battambang-Siem Reap region: 'The fields are flat and bare in the dry season, until May; they are easy to plough and are well worked, sown and harrowed directly from May. These fields are not usually marked out in regular plots.' G. Martel in her study *Lovek, village des environs d'Angkor*, Paris, EFEO 1975, describes the peasants going to observe their fields in a boat when the ears of rice emerge from above the flooded area.

[2] F. Grunewald, in an article 'Stratégies paysannes à la rescousse de l'autosuffisance: la saison agricole 1987-1988,' *Affaires cambodgiennes 1987-1988*, Paris, L'Harmattan, 1989, describes a year of comparative drought, 1987.

quick-growing rice yields a normal harvest, but unfortunately not always, for in some years not only are the rains late, but also insufficient, which also adversely affects the subsidence rice.

When the Khmers established themselves in the Angkor region, they were aware of an irrigation system based on diverting a river and its related lowest levels (this is the apparent at the important site of Sambor Prei Kuk). But on the hills and in the Siem Reap plain, where the rivers have a relatively modest flow and do not adapt to diversion, they adopted a different strategy.

From the eighth century, the Khmers began to lay out Mount Kulen, particularly on its slopes. Probably under Javanese influence, they dammed the rivers to form reservoirs (fig. 27),[3] using gravity flow to irrigate the rice fields below the dam. When they settled in the Roluos plain, they first of all constructed at Lolei a dam 3.5 km long, similar to those on Kulen, but the purpose was different; they sought a supplement to the annual flood when it was required. This implies that the water needed to be retained for some time, and consequently the undertaking should be sufficiently large to hold back water for seven to eight months. Over such a long period, much settlement occurs, which means that when the water is used it is not very rich in nutrients; the natural flood brings these essentials. The maximum level of the flood, in the Siem Reap region, of 80 cm, is generally reached in October and November.

At Lolei, because these difficulties were not foreseen, the work had to be corrected; at first, the perpendicular dykes[4] were extended, then the reservoir was completely squared off. This was sufficiently important an operation to merit being mentioned in an inscription, in the sixty-second verse of the two-sided Lolei stela.[5] Among the gifts and undertakings of Yasovarman made at the same time as the construction of the Lolei temple, there is 'this brilliant tatâka [pool] which he made himself, similar to the shape of the moon made rectangular by its creator...'. The model of the Khmer baray was born, and would only undergo very simple modifications which the Khmer collective intelligence applied, most often because of the topographical conditions of the site.

This model was established when King Indravarman had already begun the Eastern Baray, which, in its first state, was a proportional enlargement of the Lolei reservoir. The site selected at Angkor was already occupied by structures which were largely destroyed. This is the case of the Kutisvara temple, marking the site of Kuti, founded by King Jayavarman II at the beginning of the ninth century. The huge work site of this reservoir (7 km long) was only completed

---

[3] The plan in fig. 27 comes from E. Hansen, Cambodge, *Aménagement du Phnom Kulen*, UNESCO report, September 1969. He describes the Thnal Thom dam (the great dam) thus: 'This dam 310 m long, 45 m wide at its base and 5.4 m high inside, is located south-west of the village of Khla Khmum. It goes across a valley blocked at the west by a kind of promontory. The dyke seems to join the edge of this jutting terrain which marks the outlet leading to more open ground.'

[4] These details concerning the Lolei dam are based on observations made in 1966.

[5] This text was provided by Claude Jacques, to whom my sincere thanks.

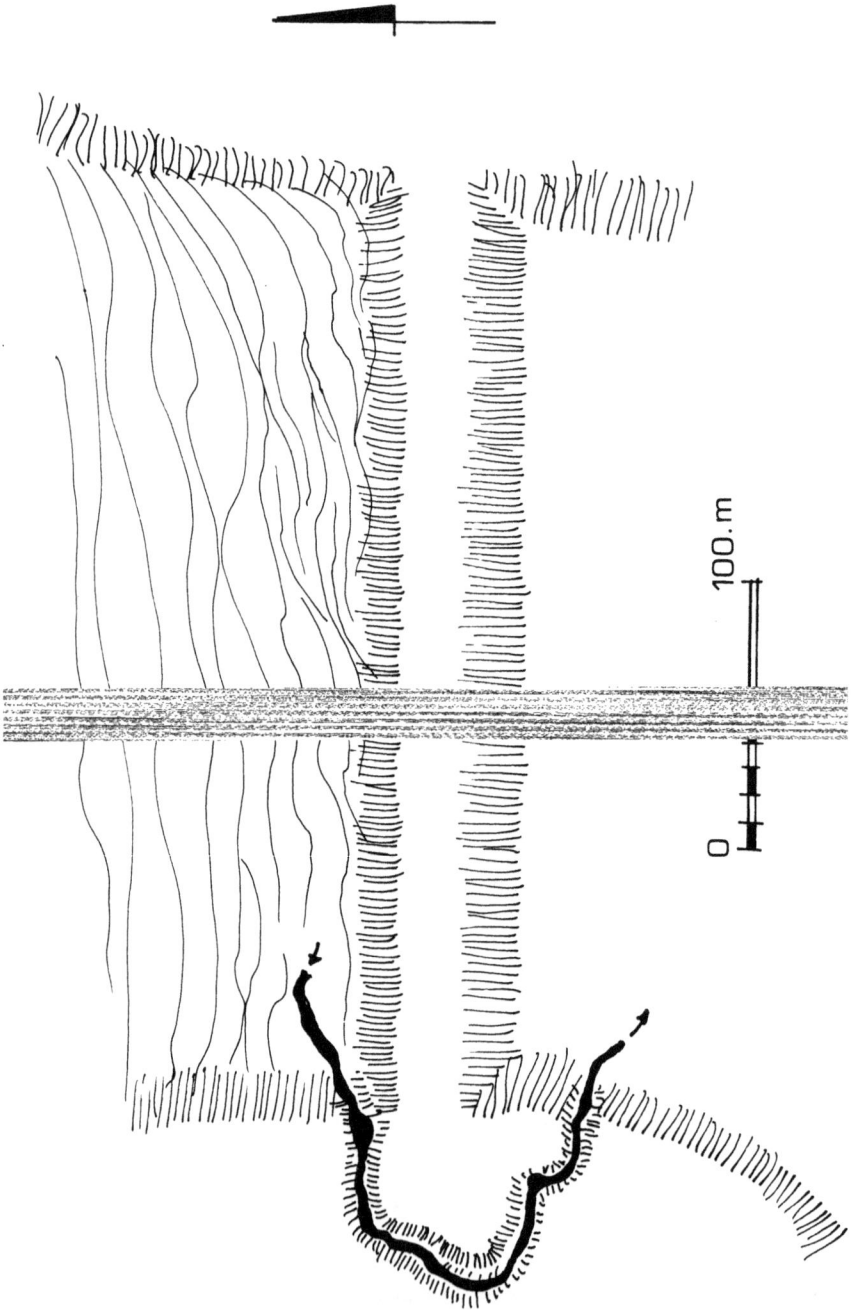

27. The Thmal Thom dam at Phnom Kulen, near Angkor, after the drawing by E. Hansen.

100. m

0

in the reign of Yasovarman, and the baray at Lolei was also transformed by this king. This is probably the reason why he attributed to himself the whole structure of the Eastern Baray in the inscriptions he had erected at the four corners of the work. The site of the baray as it can be seen today is not that which was originally laid out, but that of King Rajendravarman who undertook changes to it after his return to Angkor from Koh Ker. At Koh Ker itself, the Rahal baray, an ancient dam probably dating from the ninth century and with only three sides, was rearranged. It is probably because of weaknesses in the baray of Yasovarman that Angkor was abandoned, or else, because of the length of time needed to fill the baray with enough water, the shift to Koh Ker occurred. The Rahal dam had to be easily modified and immediately useable, but it must soon have been seen to be insufficient; it was technically retrograde, returning to the time of the Kulen settlements, and the return to Angkor was decided upon. This return involved very considerable structural work, first of all on the southern dyke of the Eastern Baray, which was shifted further south, and the island in the centre, the Eastern Mebon, was enlarged (fig. 28); on the upper level a temple dedicated to the king's ancestors was constructed, and consecrated in AD 951. It is probable that at this time the stelae at the south-east and south-west corners put up by Yasovarman were shifted to the corners of the new dyke, and all four were covered by a small pavilion of the same type as that built at the north-east corner of the Pre Rup temple.[6]

In spite of these modifications, the Eastern Baray rapidly became unusable, and the construction of a new reservoir, the Western Baray, was begun, still on the same model established at Lolei. Doubtless in order to have enough water during these new undertakings, another smaller reservoir, the Sras Srang, was constructed along the southern dyke of the Eastern Baray.[7] This undertaking does not appear today as it was first built. It was considerably modified at the end of the twelfth century at the same time as Banteay Kdei temple was built. The excavations of B.P. Groslier on the area between the reservoir and the temple show that the space between the two was filled up. The work was at first conceived as a baray in relief on the surrounding surface with, at half the height of the western dyke, a horizontal canal lined with laterite[8] (the lining measures 1.75 m at the level of the baray and 0.80 m at the slope) which ensured the distribution of the water (fig. 29) over a wider surface and supplemented the natural flooding. The remains of old dykes which could be seen, notably in the north, were markedly higher (by on average 1 m) than those to the west, with some points more than 3 m higher.

The volume of water retained in the Western Baray is almost the same as in the Eastern Baray, but the idea behind the island in the centre is very different.

---

[6] These pavilions were studied by G. Trouvé, 'Etude sur le Prei Prasat, le Prasat Komenap, et l'édicule qui abritait la stèle du baray oriental', *BEFEO*, XXXII.

[7] An important topographical drawing of the Sras Srang ensemble was published in C. Pottier and J. Dumarçay, *Documents Topographiques de la Conservation des monuments d'Angkor*, Paris, EFEO, 1993, pl.65-70. The drawing at fig.28 was based on this and some unpublished notes.

[8] Paul Courbin, *Les Fouilles du Sras Srang*, Paris, EFEO, 1989, 22, Ph. 8 and 9.

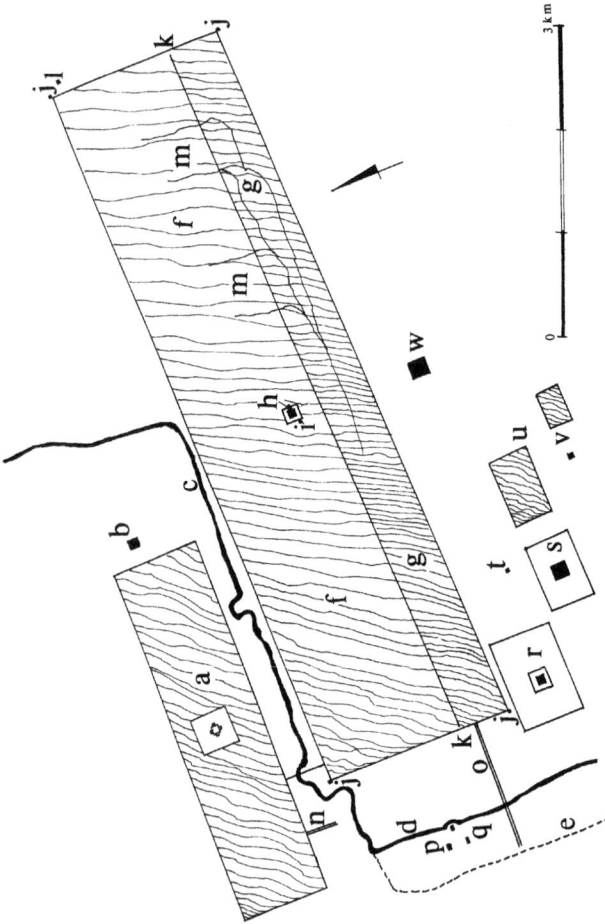

28. The Eastern Baray at Angkor: (a) the Neak Pean Baray, see also fig. 32, (b) the temple of Ta Som, (c) present course of the Siem Reap River, here using a canal going around the Eastern Baray, (d) present course of the river, where the bed is deeply cut, (e) probable course of the river before the construction of a canal which could not cut across the river, (f) original state of the Eastern Baray, (g) extension of the baray about A.D. 950, (h) original state of the Eastern Mebon, (i) extension of the Eastern Mebon about A.D. 950, (j, i, j, j) location of the Yasovarman stelae after the extension of the baray, (k, k) original location of the south-east and south-west stelae, (l) Prasat Tor, see fig.34, (m) location of the resurgence of the streams in the twelfth and thirteenth centuries, (n) a raised canal marking the end of the use of the Neak Pean baray, (o) a raised canal marking a brief re-utilization of the Eastern Baray at the end of the eleventh and beginning of the twelfth centuries, with work related to the temple of Angkor Wat marking the end of this use, (p) the Thommanon temple, (q) the Chausay Tevoda temple, and between this and Thommanon, the Spean (bridge) Thmar, built in the fifteenth century, (r) Ta Prohm temple, (s) Banteay Kedi temple, (t) Kutisvara temple, (u) the Sras Srang pool, see fig. 29, (v) Bat Chum temple and its baray, (w) Pre Rup temple.

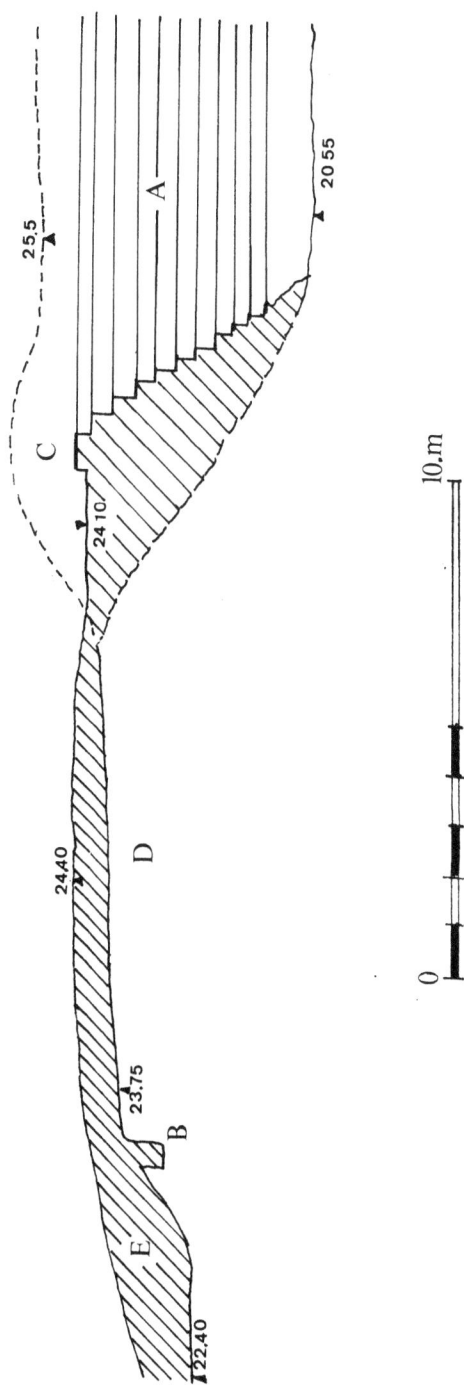

29. Cross-section of the western dyke of the Sras Srang pool, Angkor: (A) the present pool, (B) the distribution canal, built in laterite, (C) reconstituted volume of the north dyke, (D) the west dyke, (E) infill from the end of the twelfth century (contouring by the French National Geographic Institute).

It is no longer, as at Lolei or the Eastern Mebon, an ancestor temple, but a kind of 'nilometer' which indicated the exact level of water in the baray (fig.30).[9] The structure in the centre comprises a pool surrounded by a wall with openings and which has, at its axes, small towers in the form of shrines. The western one acts as an entrance to a path built on a dyke which gives access, in the centre of the pool, to a platform containing an inverse linga, something like the reflection of an upright linga, linked to the baray by a bronze pipe; using the principle of communicating vessels the level of water in the baray could be ascertained.

This was the zenith of the system the Khmers spread throughout the kingdom. For example, the new temple of Beng Melea also had a baray which was never altered (and indeed may never have been used), and which still retains much of its water delivery system, an aqueduct which crosses the dyke at its highest point (fig. 31). On the lesser sites, where flood waters could cause little damage, the Khmers built very simple reservoirs: close to Puoc near the circular city of Lovea, a small baray was built with a simple dyke 1.5 m high (fig. 32), which simply added to the flood waters when they were insufficient. When the small baray was abandoned, it became an obstacle to fields irrigated by gravitational flow, and its surface was divided into paddy fields bounded by small embankments for a different method of husbandry, whilst all around gravitation was used to distribute the natural flood, without any supplement.

When in 1181, King Jayavarman VII re-established Khmer sovereignty after the Cham invasion, the irrigation system was certainly in a very poor condition following four years of vicious warfare. One of the first concerns of the new authorities was to repair the earlier structures as much as possible. Once more the Eastern Baray was refashioned and partly filled with water in its south-west corner,[10] then new baray, still on the same model, were begun, not only at Angkor, but at new sites like Banteay Chmar. At Angkor, the new reservoir was associated with the first settlement of Jayavarman VII while his new capital, Angkor Thom, was being built. The new baray, called Neak Pean, was linked to a new architectural conception, but it was also the last time the model was used, without any other expectation of the completed work. At Neak Pean this led to serious consequences which required important modifications; in its first state the baray comprised a 2.5 m high dyke (fig. 33a), which very soon was seen to be insufficient, and was raised by 1 m. This second state[11] would have caused the temple in the central island to be flooded, so it

---

[9]   This figure, like fig.28, owes much to the observations of G. Trouvé, reported in his drawing
      of the site of Angkor, and published in _Documents Topographiques…_ op.cit., pl.1, and
      J. Dumarçay, "Notes d'architecture javanaise et khmère," _BEFEO_, LXXI, L'alimentation
      en eau du Mebon occidental.

[10] This improvement came from a partial filling of water at the end of the tenth century
      where a raised canal was built which, later, was cut when the bed of the Siem Reap River
      was changed at the time of the construction of Angkor Wat.

[11] An excavation led by a team from the World Monuments Fund, in charge of the
      restoration of Preah Khan, was conducted on the east dyke of the Neak Pean baray,

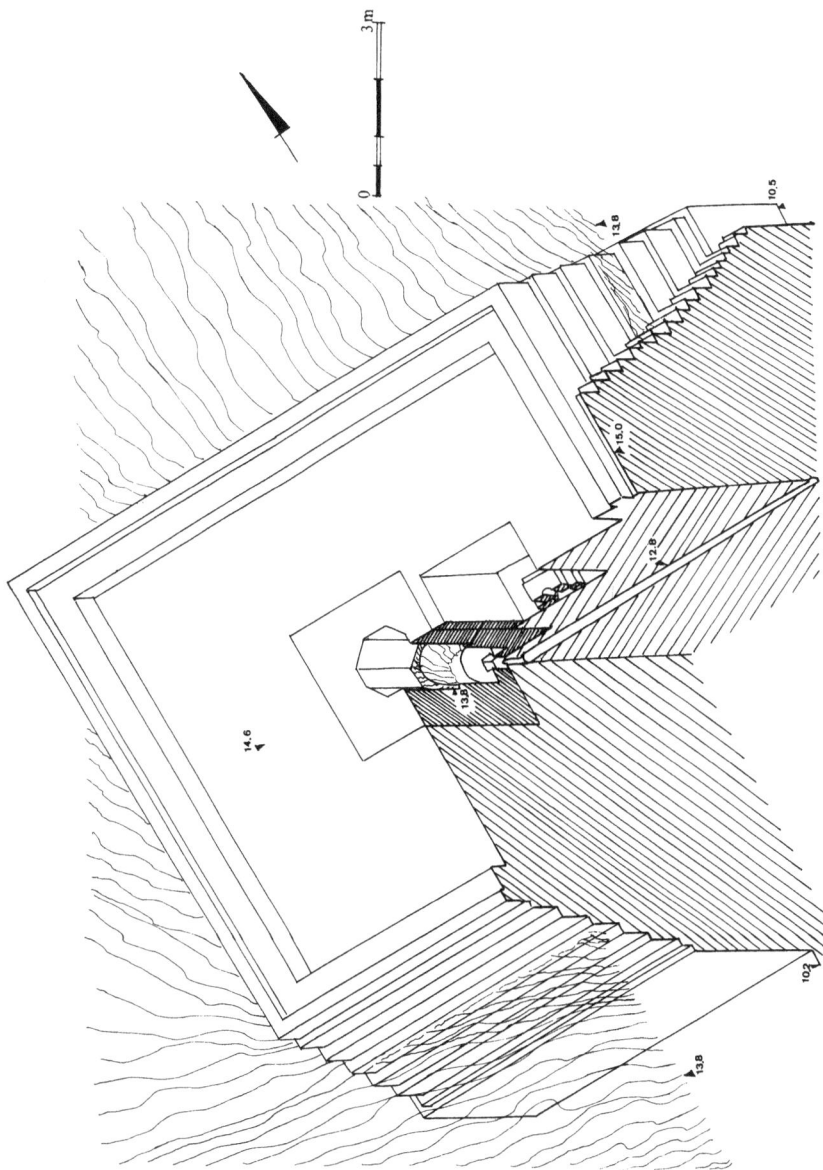

30. *Central part of the Western Mebon, Angkor (contouring by the French National Geographic Institute).*

54

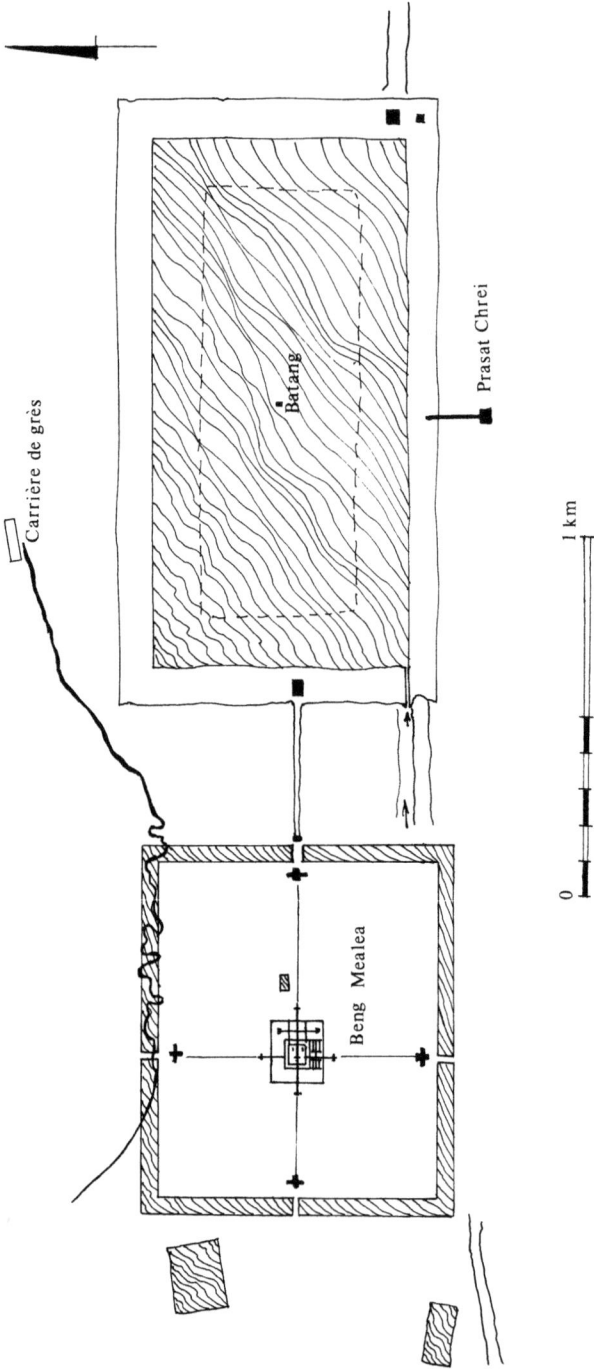

31. The temple of Beng Melea and its baray, Angkor, a sketch by E. Hansen.

Lovea

a

G

G

G

G

0   500 m

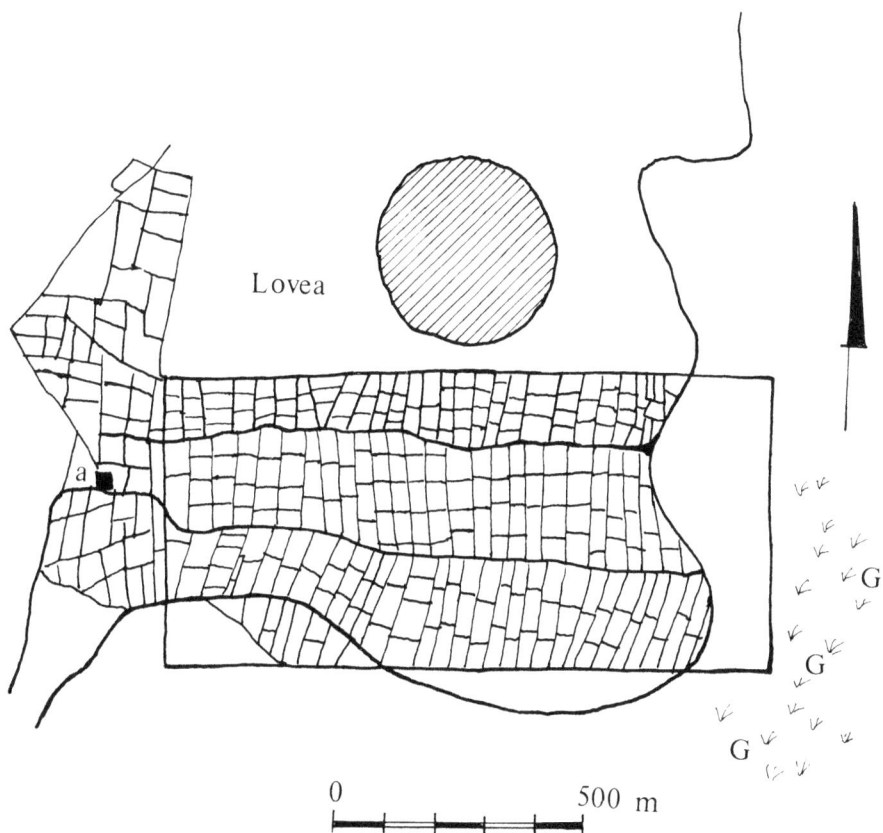

32. The baray of Puoc and the village of Lovea, Cambodia.

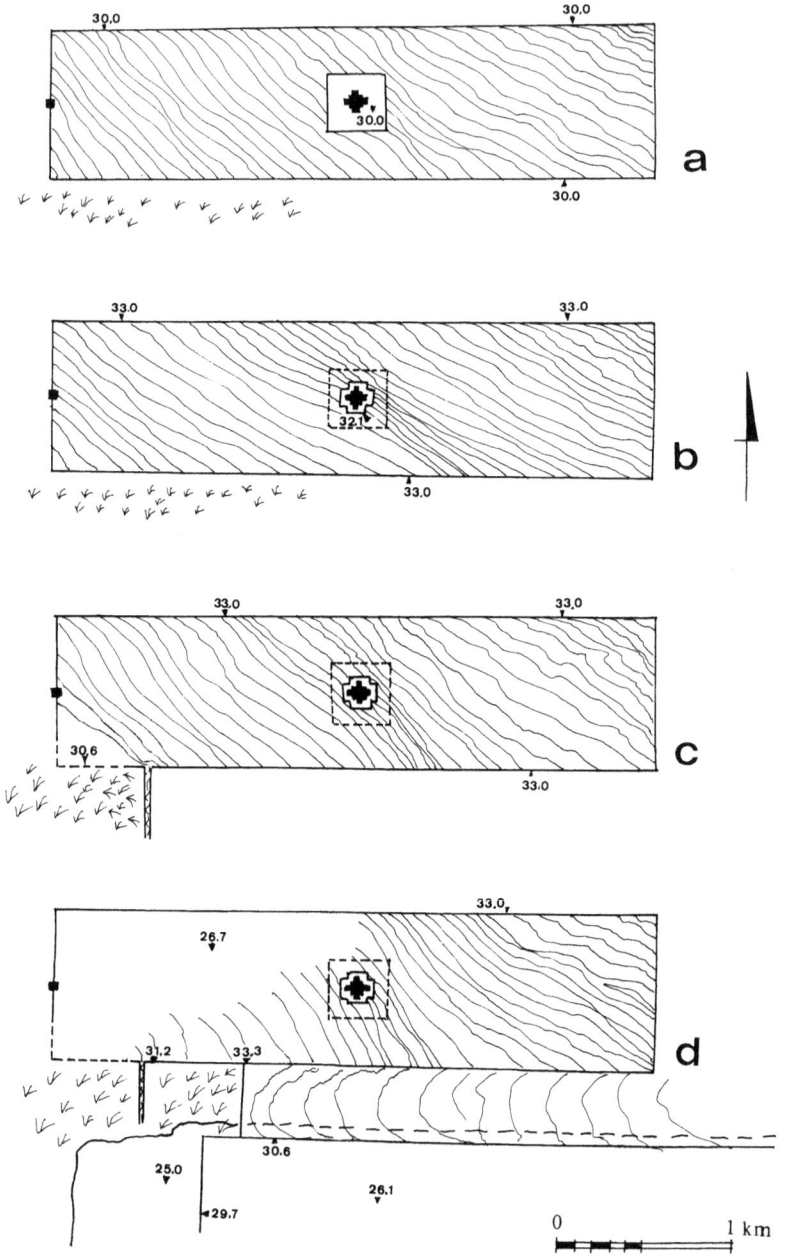

33. The four successive states of the Neak Peak baray, Angkor
(contouring by the French National Geographic Institute).

had to be protected by a surrounding dyke 1.5 m high (at the end of these works the temple of Neak Pean was below the level of the water in the baray, fig. 33b[12]). This was found to be insufficient, and a serious accident occurred; some 400 m of the dyke collapsed, or vanished under a peak flood, at the south-west corner. It is likely that the baray was abandoned for a short period and then used again in the following manner: near the collapse but in a solid part of the dyke, an opening was made which was crossed by a laterite culvert, serving to regulate the flow of the water out of the baray into a canal which provided supplementary flooding over some 200 hectares (fig. 33c). This was also abandoned when the space between the Neak Pean baray and the Eastern Baray was blocked; the Siem Reap River at that time passed under a bridge constructed along the dyke linking the two baray (probably about AD 1250). This could have lasted only a short time since, probably because of serious flooding, the river changed its course at this point and the dyke was broken (fig. 33d).

From these elements and their historical development it is possible to establish what was the model of the baray, independently of the modifications which collective intelligence brought to its different forms. Essentially the aim of these pools, in spite of the different results from their use, was to supplement the annual flood when it was insufficient. For that the baray always have the following elements: a raised dyke which ensures the retention of water, an aqueduct bringing water into the reservoir, and a parallel canal outside the dyke. The filling of this canal was probably done by cutting the dyke at its lowest point, which would allow the outflow of water for irrigation purposes by simple gravitational flow.[13] One needs to remember that the very high dykes were only meant to be used at moments of excessive flooding,[14] and usually the baray were only filled to no more than two metres, which allowed the dykes to be cut without difficulty.

When the faults in this system became too evident, probably about AD 1200, King Jayavarman VII completely changed the irrigation system,

---

at the site of the landing stage. The brief report and published drawings, in spite of their interest, provide no indications about the architectural history of the construction which, according to surface observations, seems to have two states corresponding to the two states of the dyke.

[12] It is probably because of this that it was possible to place a seated Buddha into position in the central shrine, from the navel of which came a jet of water, as Zhou Daguan (Chou Ta-kuan) related; see P. Pelliot, *Mémoires sur les coutumes du Cambodge de Tcheou Ta-kouan*, new version followed by an incomplete commentary, Paris, Maisonneuve, 1951; the most recent English edition is The Customs of Cambodia, ed. M. Smithies, Bangkok, The Siam Society, 2001, see p.20.

[13] J. Delvert, *Le paysan Cambodgien*, Paris, 1961. In this work, Professor Delvert demonstrates the extent of the survival of the technique of irrigation by gravitational flow in the 1950s.

[14] On these exceptional occasions, the temples built in the centres of the baray were completely covered by water.

abandoning the construction of great reservoirs and changing all the bridges on the road system to the same model (fig. 34).[15] Many of these new constructions, while serving the flow of water and land transport, acquired a new function, of being a dam. Water no longer flowed from the surface of the land, and generally the principal of gravitational flow was abandoned, resulting in the construction of a network of canals and the use of means of raising the water to the level of the paddy fields. It was thus at this period that the network of canals appeared which were dug into the earth and which appear in aerial photographs.

Still more than the baray, the model of the dam-bridges had to be adapted to the topography of the site by the collective intelligence of the Khmers, but, whatever the site, the basic form is perfectly recognizable. The volume of water retained clearly depends on the surrounding relief. A relatively modest bridge, like the Spean Tor, but profiting by the old dyke of the Eastern Baray (fig. 35) can retain almost a million cubic metres of water, whereas the important bridge built near Kompong Kdei, the Spean Prap Tos (fig. 36) only holds back 350,000 cubic metres.[16] The use of the reservoir at Spean Tor combined the old techniques of the baray with the new ones of the bridge; the water in the reservoir is fed into the external eastern canal of the Eastern Baray which allows it to be distributed by a simple outflow providing irrigation by gravitation in the east-west direction, because of the local topography dominated by Phnom Bok, 217 m high. But whatever the volume of the water retained, the person in charge of its distribution was very powerful, and rivalled that of the capital. This had its disadvantages, in particular when it became necessary to carry out repairs. These bridges were not strong and often subject to violent spates in the river; in these cases the streams often carried the tree trunks which had fallen from the river banks, and which crashed against the bridge piles, sometimes causing serious damage, the repair of which could not be assured locally by the revenue obtained from the distribution of water. The weakened central powers were no longer in a position to subsidize these repairs and gradually the system of bridge-dams disappeared, though a few survived. In the sixteenth century, when the site of Angkor was revived, the bridge located at the axis of the so-called Gate of Victory was destroyed, and rebuilt according to the model, probably with the same function as a bridge-dam, but perhaps with another purpose than rice cultivation, namely fishing. Upstream from this bridge, on the north bank, there are numerous pools which could only be filled when the river was in flood; when the water level went down, the fish were trapped in the pools. This method of catching fish is still generally used today, not at this spot, as the river has dug too deeply into the ground, but downstream, where the topography is more favourable.

When the member of the Chinese embassy, Zhou Daguan, went to Cambodia

---

[15] The map in fig.34 owes much to the as yet unpublished work of B. Bruguier, to whom my thanks.

[16] The Spean Prap Tos was the subject of a topographical study in *Documents topographiques...op.cit.*, pl.72.

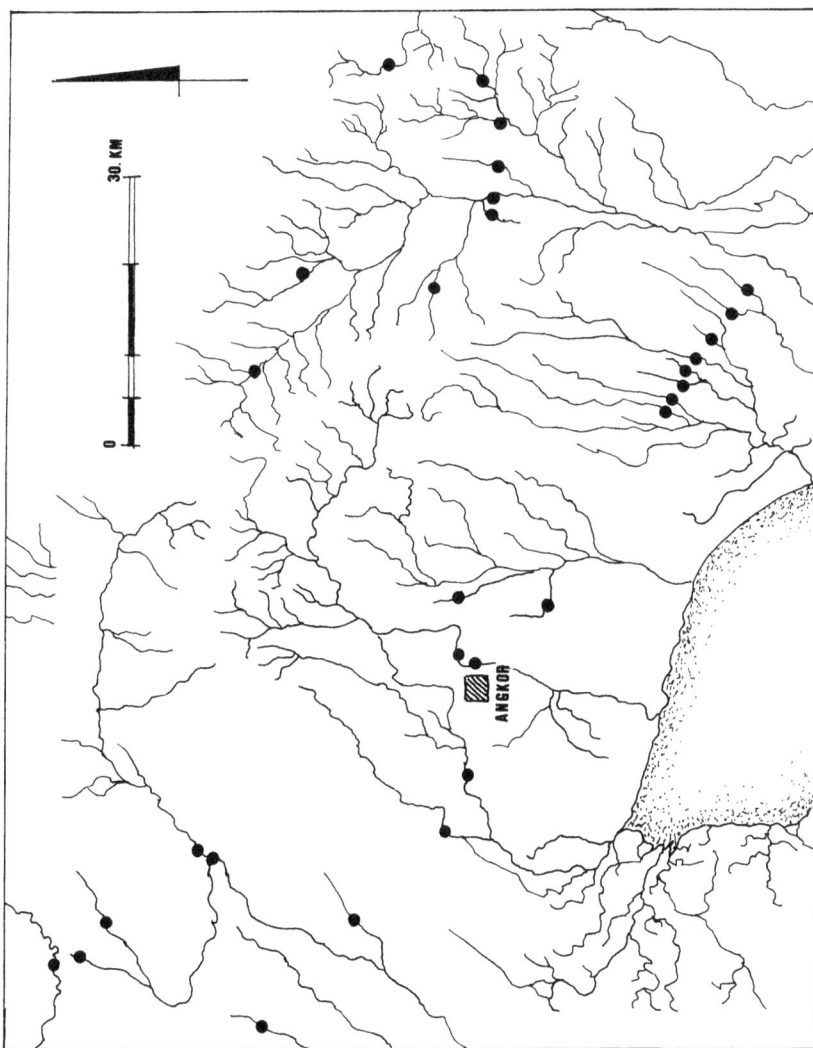

34. *Location of the bridges in Cambodia constructed at the end of the twelfth century (following the indication of B. Brugier).*

60

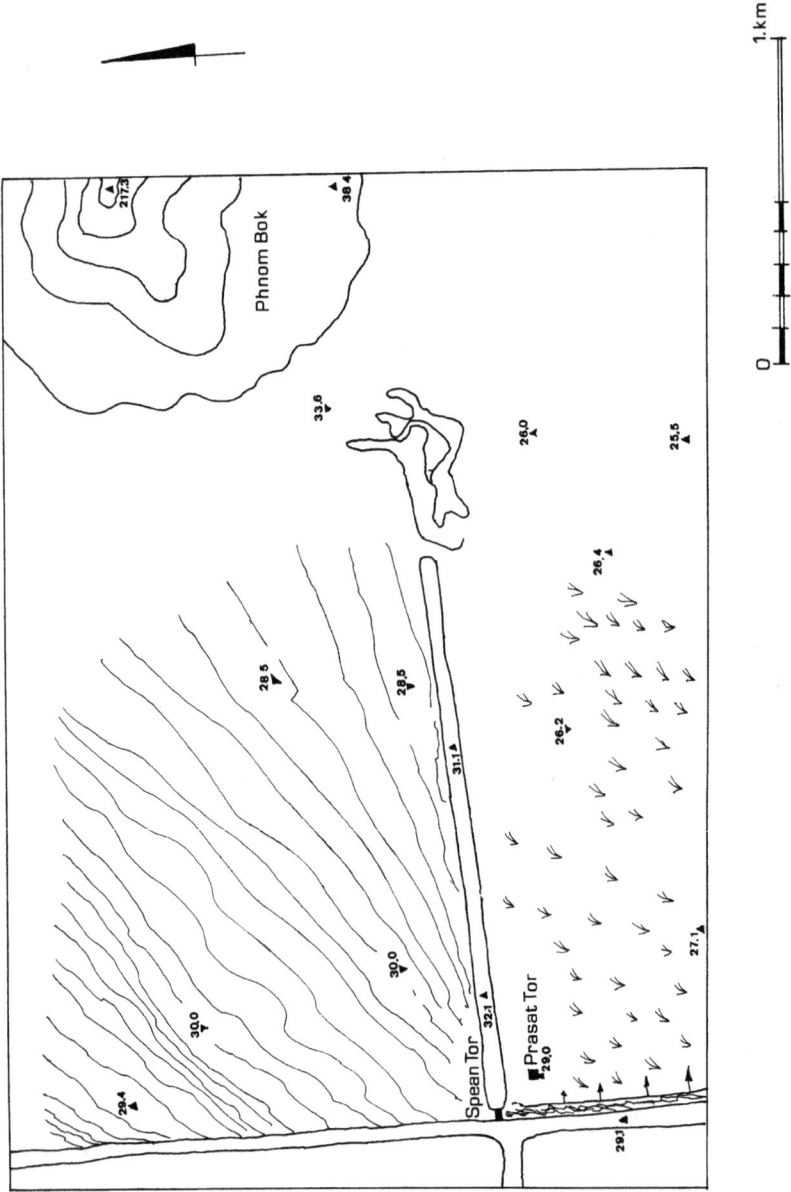

35. *Location of the area of water retained behind the Spean Tor, Cambodia (contouring by the French National Geographic Institute).*

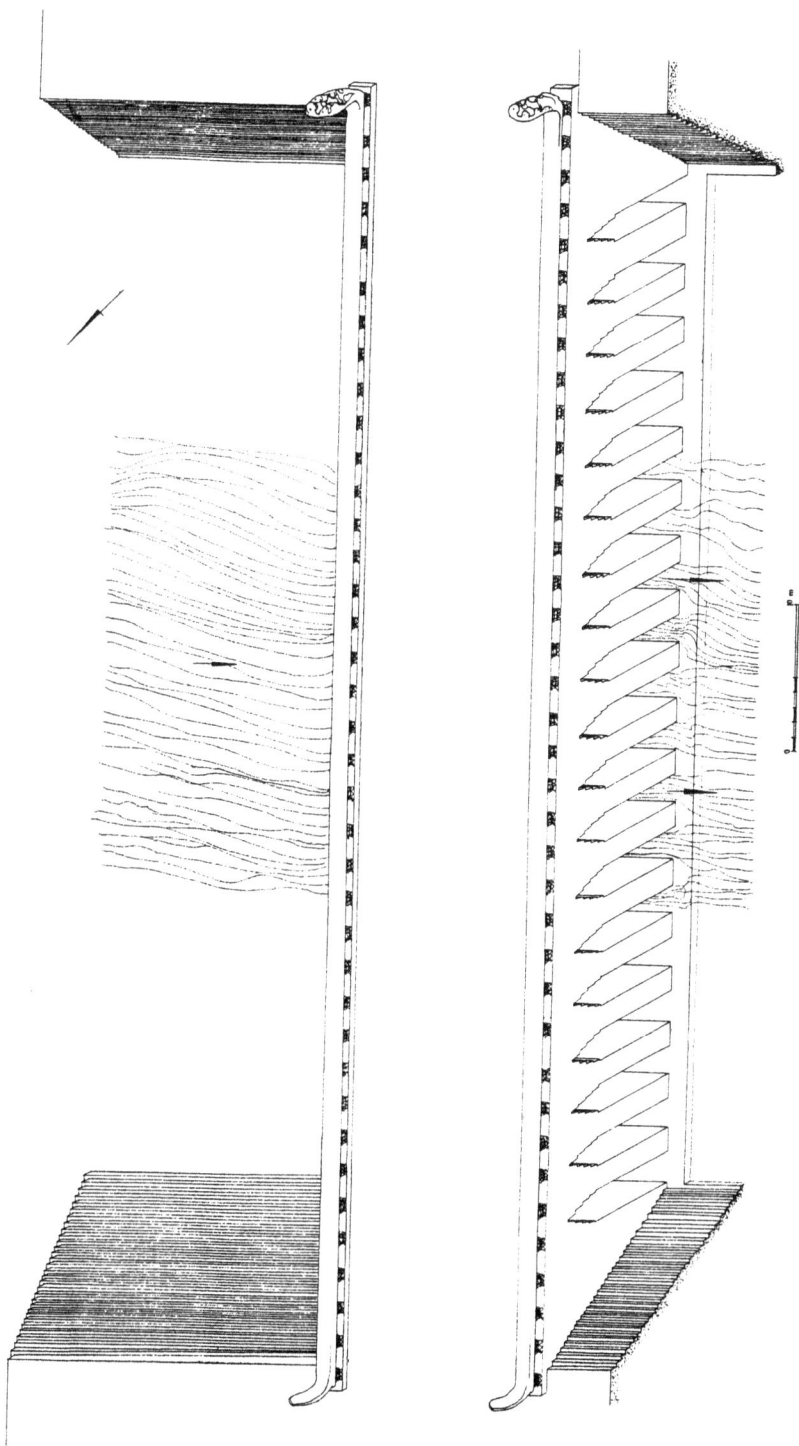

36. Axonometric drawing of the Spean Prap Tos, Cambodia.

in AD 1296-1297, he related 'the eastern lake is ten li to the east of the walled city, and about one hundred li in circumference. In the middle is a stone tower with stone chambers. In the tower is a bronze sleeping Buddha, from whose navel water flows uninterruptedly. The northern lake is five li to the north of the walled city. In the middle is a square golden tower, and several dozen stone chambers. Concerning the golden lion, the golden Buddha, the bronze elephant, and bronze ox and bronze horse, all are found there.'[17] The northern lake has been identified as Neak Pean, which still retained some water when Zhou Daguan visited Angkor. As for the eastern lake, G. Coedes thinks that Zhou Daguan made an error and was thinking of the Western Baray. I do not share this view since at that time the Western Baray was dry,[18] but the Eastern Baray still had water in its south-west corner, largely because of the resurgence of streams which occurred to the south of the dyke of the first state (fig. 28).

Zhou Daguan describes agriculture in a subsequent section where he possibly evokes irrigation by gravitation which was still being practiced at the time of his visit: 'there exist sorts of natural fields where rice grows without being sown; when the water reaches a fathom in height, the rice grows likewise; I think this must be a special variety'. Rice grown using gravitational irrigation had a maximum stalk of 90 cm, the ear included, and, as Zhou Daguan remarks, its growth follows the rise in water level even when this is rapid. Of course, the Chinese traveller is mistaken in thinking that it does not have to be sown, but it seems, from the brevity of his note, that this technique was hardly used much, or perhaps not at all, which would explain why he thought the rice could be grown without being sown. He is perhaps describing the oriza sativa flutens variety, which grows in tandem with the rise in water level.[19]

A recent study[20] attributes the decline of Angkor to geological phenomena, in particular a rise in the level of the soil in the historic period. The author takes as his chief example the hollowing out of the Siem Reap River parallel to the east wall of Angkor Thom. This particularity, noted by several scholars, could only have occurred after the construction of the bridge in the axis of the Gate of Victory at Angkor Thom, that is, after the sixteenth century. If this

---

[17] Zhou Daguan, *The Customs of Cambodia*, ed. M. Smithies, Bangkok, The Siam Society, 2001, 20.

[18] Although the reservoir and aqueducts were still in a good state of preservation at the time of Zhou Daguan, they were too when the Spaniard Bartolomo de Argensola at the end of the sixteenth century (B.P. Groslier, *Angkor et le Cambodge au XVIe siècle*, Paris, PUF, 1957, 79: 'the aqueducts, although dry, are no less splendid'). His text was published in AD 1609. The baray no longer functioned and was replaced by a reservoir dammed by a bridge near the north-east corner of the baray.

[19] In a 1931 report of rice cultivation in Indochina, cited above, it is noted that 'the plant, already strong with the arrival of the water, grows quickly enough to follow the regular rise in water level'.

[20] Heng L. Thung, 'Geohydrology and the decline of Angkor,' *Journal of the Siam Society*, 82/1&2, 1994. My thanks to my colleague Olivier de Bernon for bringing my attention to this article.

geological phenomenon were confirmed, it would certainly be a reason for the final abandonment of Angkor.

Sometimes it has been asked why the Khmers, having observed the (comparatively relative) indifferent functioning of the baray, stayed so long with the system.[21] This is inherent in the use of a model of whatever type. Another example of the persistence of the use of a given form is even longer, that of houses using sagging beam constructions, mentioned earlier. The most ancient form of this type of house dates form the beginning of the Christian era, and it is still being used today. The technique of sagging roof ridges gives a very large internal volume, free of all timber supports for the roof. When it was no longer possible to construct these houses with the original techniques (because the great boles found in the local forests had become rare), the form was still adhered to but the technique was changed. The collective intelligence of each group of humans using these house forms filled the internal volume with a structure which could support the roof, the outwardly inclined gables became an image and had no technical purpose, but everything which formerly was of interest in these houses for their inhabitants, their internal volume, was lost, and that because they failed to anticipate a new architectural form. The same is true of the baray which, failing to envisage a different form, the collective intelligence of the Khmers was content to adapt the model created at Lolei to the topography of the sites.

---

[21] B.P. Groslier, when excavating near the Thommanon temple in 1964-65, cleared the bridge there, the Spean Thmar. It could be seen that it was built on a laterite foundation raft of an older bridge which was probably made of wood. The stone bridge, judging from the numerous blocks reutilized in the masonry, must have been a late construction, no doubt dating from the re-occupation of Angkor in the sixteenth century. A topographical drawing of the surroundings of Spean Thmar, after the excavations of B.P. Groslier was published in *Documents topographiques...op.cit.*, pl.49. This drawing shows the different levels of construction; the foundation raft of the first bridge is at a height of 17.60m, the sixteenth century bridge at a height of 18.15m, the level of the old road 20.40, and that of the modern road approximately 21.50, and the river 12.60; the hollowing out from the foundation raft of the sixteenth century at this point is 5.55m.

III

THE SUCCESSIVE MODELS OF
THE SAME MONUMENT

Because of historical events, accidents, or the mere antiquity of buildings, some monuments were redesigned, sometimes extensively, following models which were adapted to existing forms. This is the case with Borobudur, the architectural history of which follows the religious and political changes which transformed central Java from the end of the eighth to the beginning of the ninth centuries. The monument was made to conform with this evolution, following successive plans which all left their heteroclite traces, giving Borobudur its unusual appearance. The different forms were almost always seen to be replicated and numerous scholars, from P. Mus[1] to J. de Casparis,[2] have commented on the duality of the monument, which Mus summarized as 'a stepped pyramid in a stupa'.

The stepped pyramid was laid out on the initiative of the Hindu Sanjaya dynasty about AD 775, following a model whose origin is not easy to determine, but, because of the use of perspective effects, was probably Indian. To increase the height of the pyramid, everything which could not be seen from the ground around the structure was eliminated, as, for example, with the base of the retaining wall of the second level (fig. 37). This principle of eliminating elements which could not be seen from possible viewpoints appeared in the south of India and was already completely mastered during the Pallava period. Also with the desire to enlarge the structure, the cornice is disproportionate, being higher than necessary, designed in relation to the proposed height of the wall; the diminution in the width of the stairways, as one climbs up the monument, corresponds to this. Under the influence of the Buddhist Sailendra dynasty, the Sanjaya abandoned their construction, and the pyramid was incomplete; only the first two levels were in position as well as the stairways giving access to them. In spite of this fragmentary state, the structure was of such a size that it could not fail to evoke the importance of Hinduism,[3] so the Sailendra decided, about AD 795, to adapt the part of the building already constructed to be the base of a huge stupa, a proven model, which was widely used throughout South-East Asia and much of southern Asia until the thirteenth century (fig. 38).

When they began work on this site, the Sailendra already had some experience of modifying structures; they had shifted from what was probably a fairly rigorous form of Buddhism to that of the five Jina, and had, for these new

---

[1]   P.Mus, *Barabudur, esquisse d'une histoire du bouddhisme fondé sur la critique archéologique des textes*, reprinted New York, Arno Press, 1978.

[2]   J.G. de Casparis, *Prasasti Indonesia I*, Bandung, 1950.

[3]   *Candi Sewu...* op.cit., chapter VI.

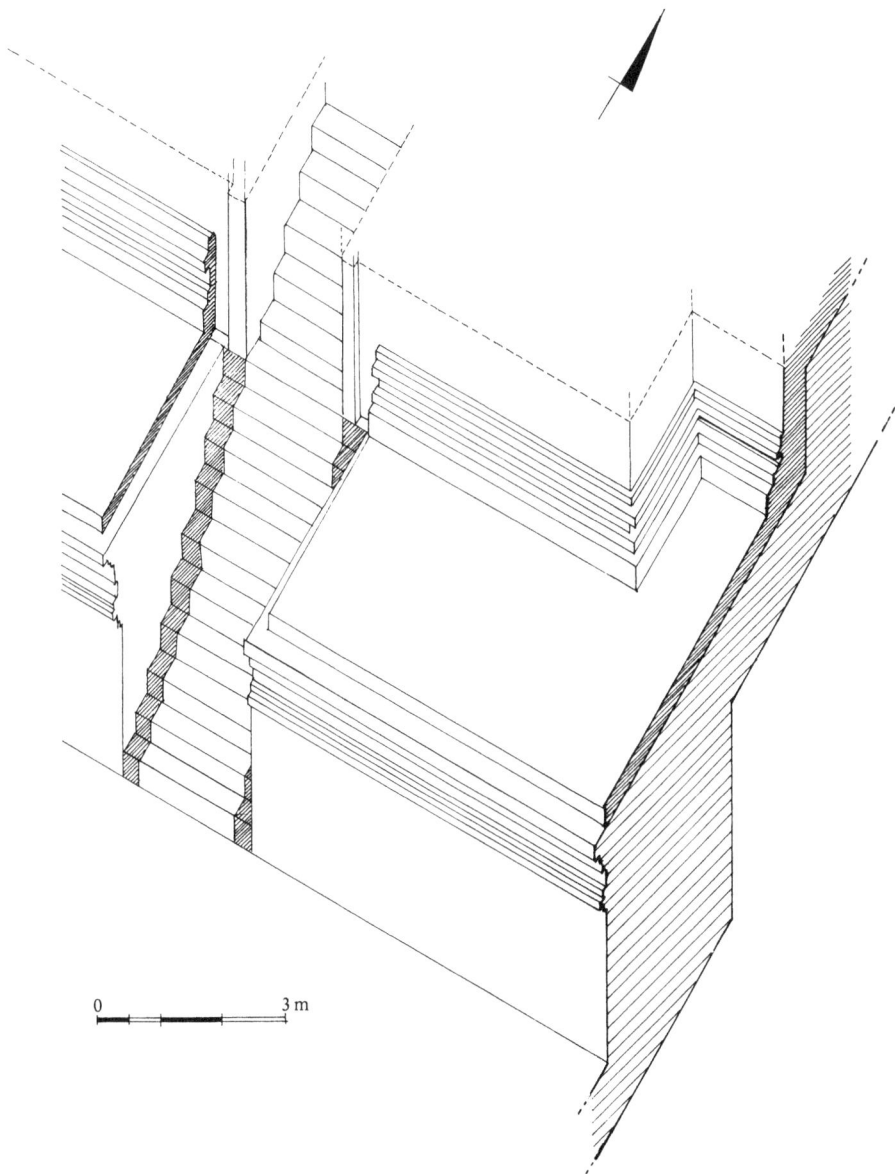

37. *Suppression of the perspective effects at the second state of Borobudur.*

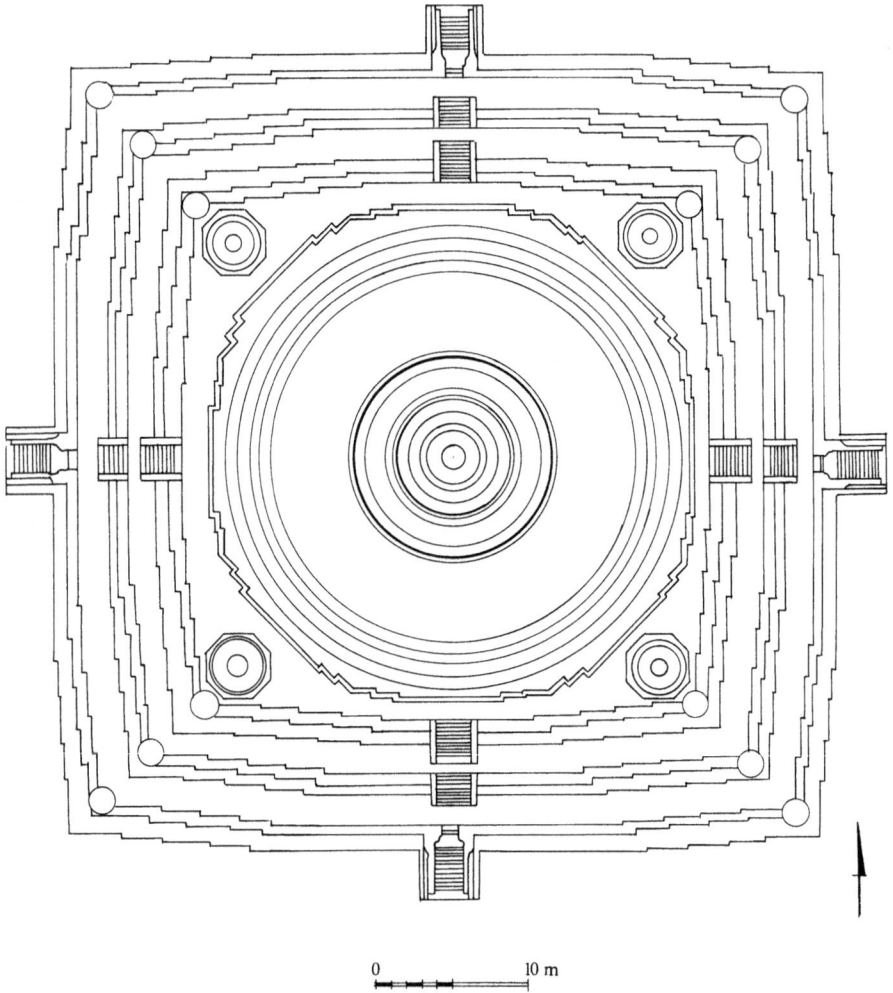

0   10 m

38. Probable model of the topmost stupa of the second state of Borobudur.

rites considerably changed the temple of their capital, Candi Sewu. The end of the first stage of these works, never entirely completed, is indicated by an inscription, unfortunately of little significance, dated AD 792. At Borobudur, the model of the stupa was adapted to the form of the pyramid, without there being any consideration of the completed structure other than that guaranteed by the model selected, but when the structure was almost complete, a part of it collapsed.

The collapse chiefly affected the north side and all the superstructure, notably the terminal stupa. Work was immediately resumed, but with a new model, the origins of which W. Stutterheim,[4] taking into account the architectural history of Borobudur, probably discovered. All the difficulties faced by applying the most recent model (which largely explains the criticism Stutterheim's thesis provoked) come from the fact that it was impossible to go back, given the huge mass of construction work already completed. In these difficult circumstances, the master builder could not follow the selected model with its complex meaning, except in the final stage of the monument, where the destruction was so great that there was barely anything left standing on an open space. Subsequent work comprised only additions which did not materially change the form of the monument.

At Borobudur, three successive models were employed: the first was abandoned because of political events, the second because of the partial collapse of the structure, the third because the model was adapted to an already well-advanced structure. In each case it was a matter of adapting to the site, and so Borobudur became a work adapted to the circumstances, and was almost accidental (as demonstrated in the partial collapse). It can be seen how the model conditions some of the architecture, but the structure also reflects the imposition of human authority. With the second state of the monument there is a break with Hinduism, as with the suppression of all the perspective effects, unifying the width of the flights of stairs (fig.37), and introducing a base to the walls of the first level, without taking into account the volume of the cornice. The Sailendra completely enveloped the work of the conquered Sanjaya by eliminating everything which explicitly recalled the Hindu origins of the structure.

The choice of model for the third state, although largely due to circumstances, probably had some political overtones. The theories expressed by the monument in that state, as determined by Stutterheim, would not have been accessible to many. On the other hand, the choice of the second state is what one expects of a stupa; it has to allow the rites to be performed, especially the circumambulation, which the final state still had to permit. But the symbolic effect was completely different, only understood by the educated, by the aristocracy. When the Hindus reunified central Java (about AD 830), they re-appropriated the monuments without difficulty, at the expense of some minimal changes, but which incorporated some cultural elements, both religious

---

4   W.F. Stutterheim, *Studies in Indonesian Archaeology*, The Hague, 1956, Chandi Borobudur, name, form, and meaning.

and technical, they had recently received from India. For example, the transformation of the entrance doorways to the first gallery was made using the
technique of a double stone dressing placed over an indifferent infill. But to
show that Hinduism had again become the dominant religion, a temple dedicated to the Trimurti, Candi Banon, was laid out (also about AD 830) inside
the area given over to Borobudur.

The changes from one state to another, conforming to a new type, appear
in very many monuments, and each time occur by adapting the newly selected
model to the site and the existing structures. For example, in Wat Phu (a
Khmer temple dating from the eighth to thirteenth centuries, located near
Champassak in southern Laos) the main temple followed a rectangular plan
(fig. 39) then currently used in what is called Funan art at Sambor Prei Kuk or
at Prasat Andet, but when a square plan was used at Kulen[5] and subsequently
at Roluos, possibly inspired by Javanese temples, the shrine of Wat Phu, built
in brick, was transformed. It was not possible to shift from the initial rectangle
to a square, but on the new plan, the axes were much more prominent. To
adapt the shrine to the current fashion, this slight change was sufficient (fig. 40,
building A), and, probably a little later, at the beginning of the twelfth century
the temple was further modified: a long sandstone building was added (fig.
40, B).[6] This new form was used on the site at Angkor, during one stage of
the construction of Thommanon and Chausay Tevoda. Not far from Wat Phu
a new temple at Nang Sida was built on the extended model of Wat Phu (fig.
41). From this example it can be seen how the transformation of a structure
by the accumulation of different forms ends up by creating a new coherent
structure; Nang Sida is the unified expression of all the changes in nearby
Wat Phu. It was also at this period that the orientation given to shrines was
fixed; they should face east. This was impossible at Wat Phu, since the site
was laid out on the broadest slope of the mountain in order to obtain a proper
functioning of the baray at the bottom and related pools. There had to be a
rapid change to the original orientation (in the twelfth century), in conformity
with the lie of the land.

At Candi Badut, dating from the eighth century, in the east of Java, the
superposition of three different states can be seen. The first is similar to
temples of the same period built on the Dieng plateau, without being strictly
identical, in particular in relation to the volume, which is large in east Java.
From this detail it can be seen that one is dealing with a common model (giving

---

[5] At Kulen, the rectangular plan was used at Prasat Neak Ta, where the reference to Sambor
    Prei Kuk is found in the reductions of the building decorating the façades (P. Stern, 'Le
    style des Kulen,' *BEFEO* XXXVIII, 1938, 111-49, ph.LXXI). In the same article Stern
    offers very convincing arguments for the Javanese origin of some of the decoration on
    the Kulen monuments. The pyramid of Koh Ker has a square plan but with a project-
    ing stairway, which gives it an oblong layout, probably dating to before the temporary
    abandonment of Angkor in the tenth century.

[6] The temple would be changed again, at an unknown date, by the addition of the small
    shrine at the side of the entrance (C in fig.40).

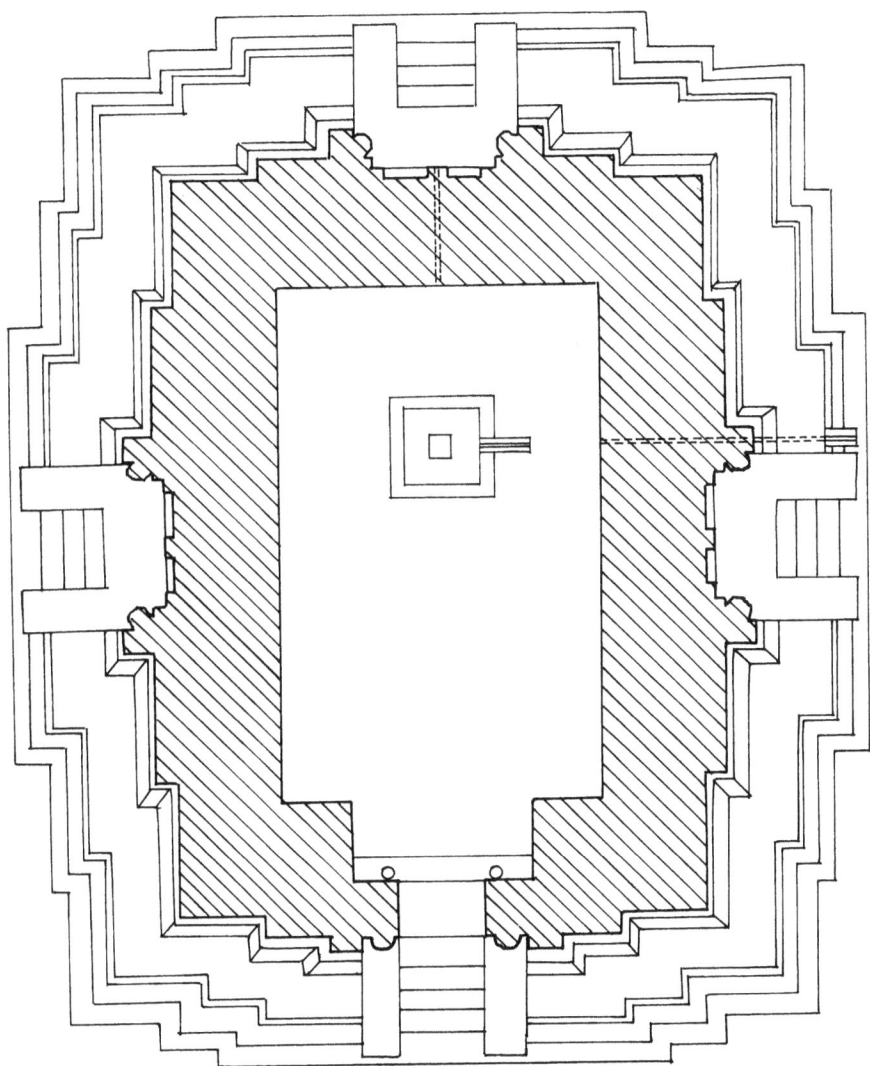

*39. Reconstituted plan of the original plan of the temple
at Wat Phu, southern Laos.*

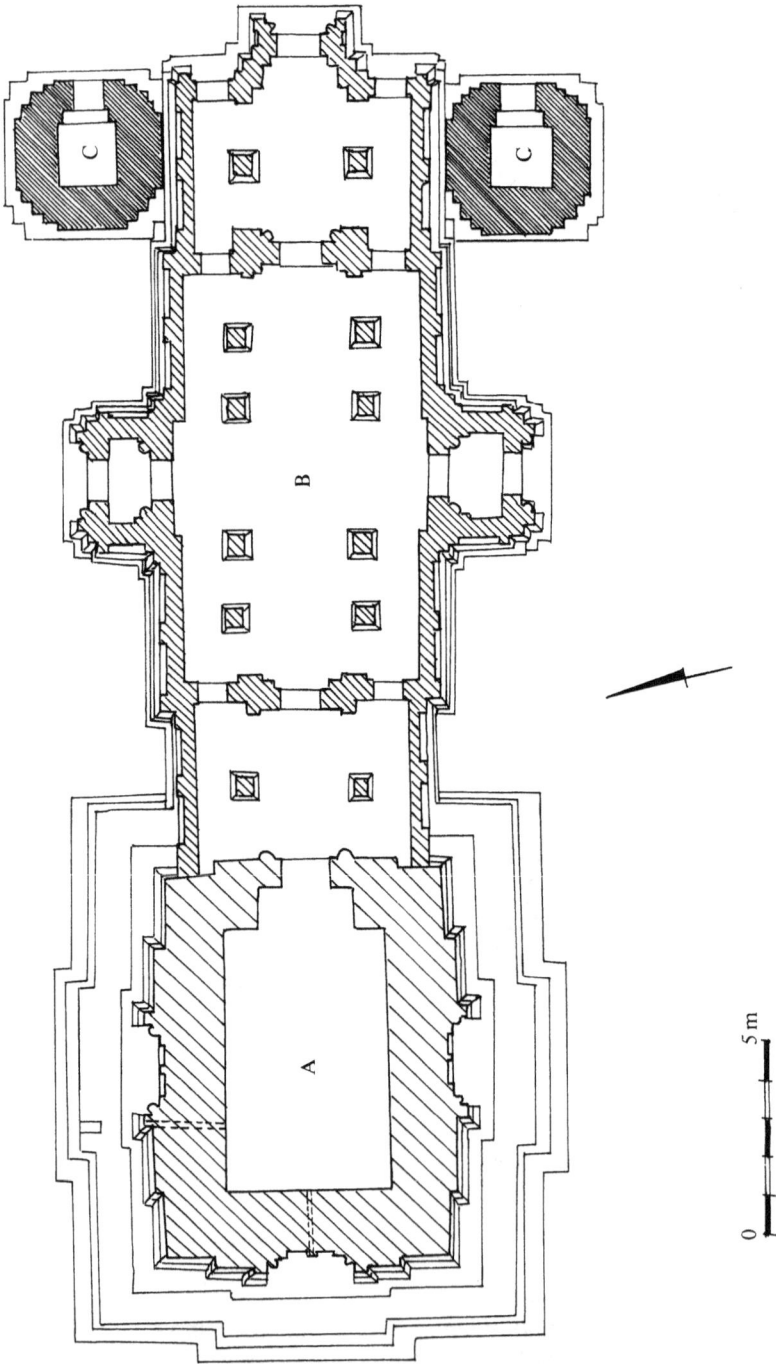

40. *Plan of the present state of Wat Phu; (A) the brick temple, (B) sandstone additions (C) two small brick shrines, now destroyed.*

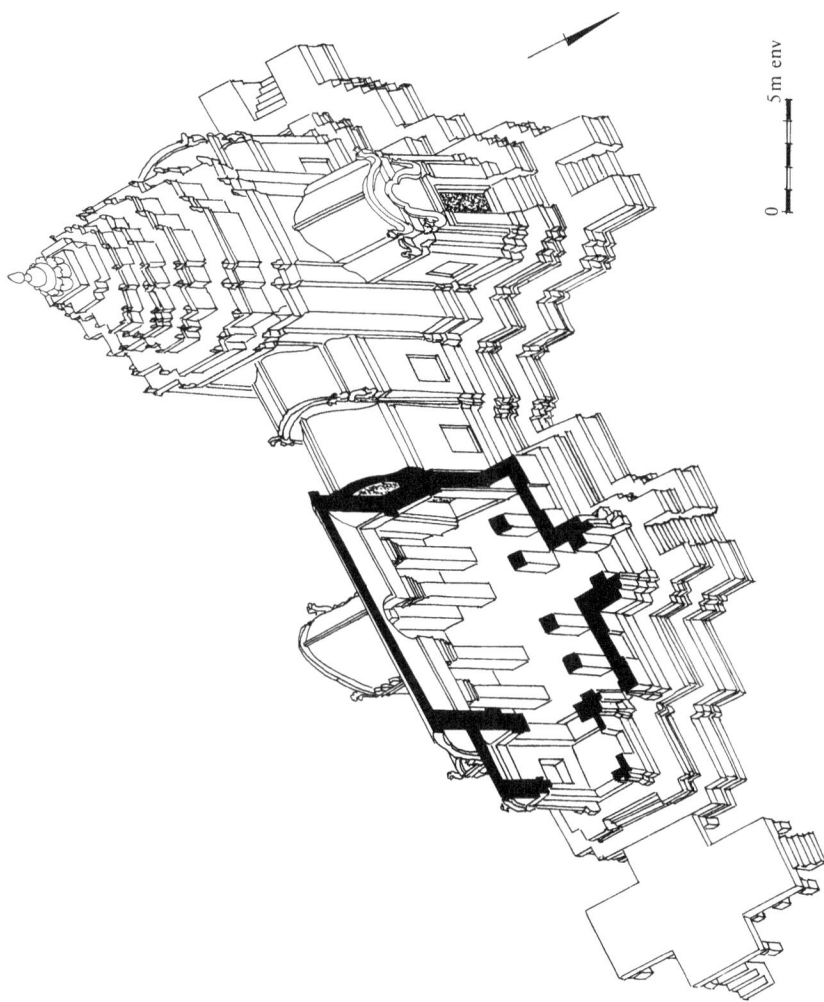

41. *Axonometric reconstitution of the temple of Nang Sida, southern Laos.*

0   5 m env

the proportions but not the dimensions),[7] and not a copy of a pre-existing structure. At the beginning of the ninth century, the second wave of Hindu influence brought to Java previously unknown techniques of construction and laying out, leading to a renewal of a number of temples. At Candi Badut, the structure itself was hardly touched (just the niches of the different façades were changed), but the attempt was made to give the space inside the shrine the appearance of having been conceived with an eye to the new rituals of laying out, leaving the centre free of any building. It was not possible to move the temple, so the enclosure and the entrance pavilion were modified, providing a new space where the centre was not covered, making the site conform to the new schema.[8] Finally in the thirteenth century, when the kings of east Java had abandoned their religious initiatives, handing over all power to the religious authorities, be they Buddhist or Hindu, the reduction in economic resources made modifications more common to bring old shrines up to date. This was also the case at Candi Badut, the superstructures of which were refashioned by inserting miniature temples between those already in position, and which probably produced a silhouette comparable to those of the original shrines nearby.

On each of these monuments one can see that the structures were refashioned according to mode of the day, but when one looks at all these changes, and the buildings erected contemporaneously, one can discern a desire to leave one's trace, and sometimes architecture becomes the expression of a kind of reassertion of power over the population. For example, when in the ninth century Hinduism and Buddhism competed with each other in central Java, there was a particularly sensitive geographical area where the two religions faced each other (fig. 42). About AD 830, when Hinduism was re-established throughout central Java, outside this area of confrontation, a sufficiently self-evident manifestation of Buddhism like Borobudur could be allowed to survive (with, though, a re-appropriation shown in some additions), but, where the conflict was particularly acute, work sites were interrupted and abandoned (as at Candi Bogan). Then a complete construction campaign was hastily undertaken; new techniques permitted a rapid execution of the building programme but they also caused many collapses. So the site of the double temples of Candi Perot and Pringapus includes remains of an ensemble which was probably as important as Candi Prambanan.

In the capital itself, Candi Sewu was unfinished and would never be completed; it was abandoned. Close by, to mark triumphant Hinduism, Candi Prambanan was built, dedicated to the Trimurti; its vast size proclaimed better than anything else the unambiguous strength of the conquerors. Furthermore

---

[7] Even when the model is described in the treatises, the dimensions are not stated. This leads to their universality, as the building can be constructed according to local conditions and the master builders knew for sure, from experience, that the system of measures could vary considerably from one place to another.

[8] J. Dumarçay, *Le savoir des maîtres d'oeuvre javanais du XIIIe et XIVe siècles*, Paris, EFEO, 1986.

73

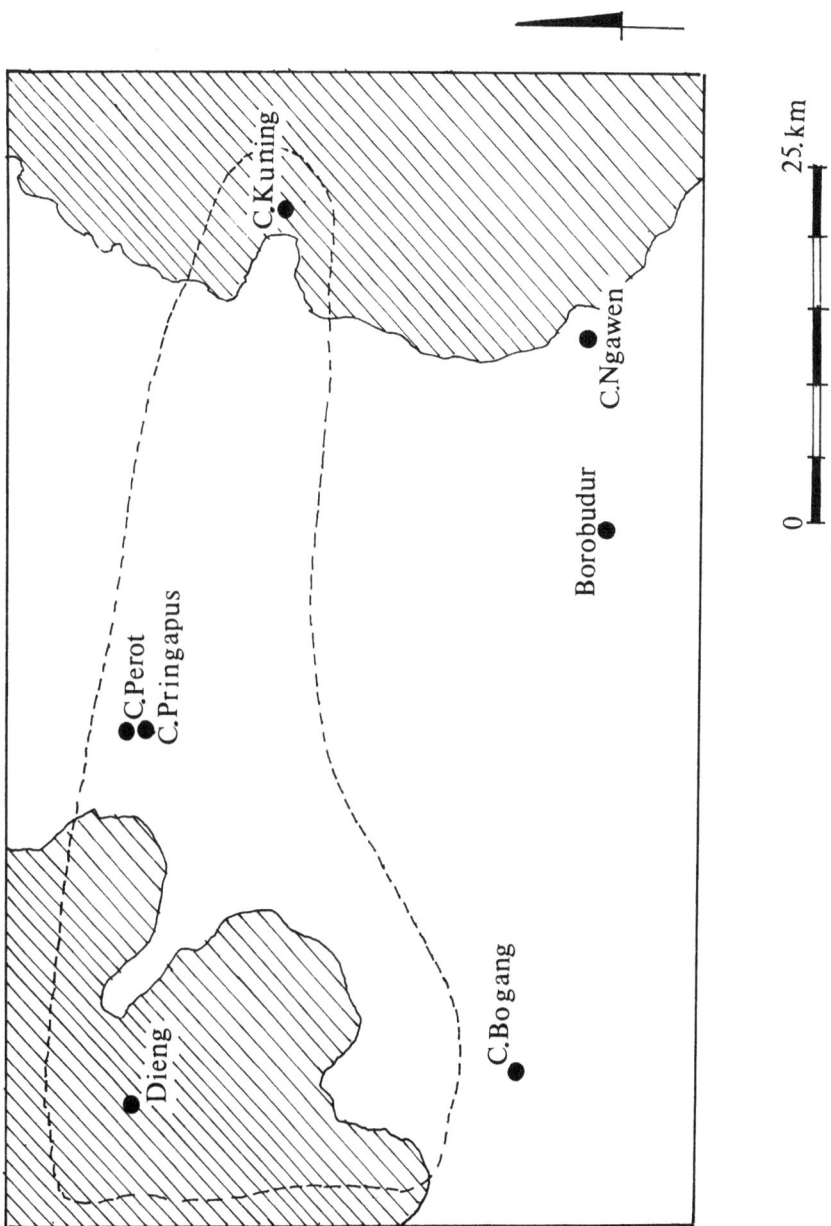

42. *The chief area of confrontation between Hinduism and Buddhism in central Java from the seventh to the ninth centuries.*

when the new powers built a Buddhist temple, Candi Plaosan, probably to satisfy the Buddhist aristocracy, it was on a model taking up the concept of an ideal geography of the kingdom, similar to that at the huge Hindu temple close by. Inscriptions on each of the small structures surrounding the two main sanctuaries at Plaosan indicate the name of the person commissioning the building, his place of residence or the place where he exercised his authority.[9] These buildings, identical in plan and elevation, were either given freely, or else under constraint, with the central authorities expressing in this way their power.

In the Khmer empire, the monuments sometimes underwent similar transformations, with an accumulation of plans from different sources. This was particularly evident at Phimeanakas,[10] which was conceived at a time when the oblong plan was in vogue (probably in the second half of the eighth century; see Chapter I) and it was to serve as the central temple of a town or, more exactly, a large settlement. At this period, the upper terrace was occupied by a wooden gallery probably surrounding a shrine built on a high foundation, dominating the ensemble. The second state was contemporary with the reign of King Jayavarman V (AD 968-1001), when he ordered the construction of the enclosure of the royal palace and the entrance pavilions. The inscription allowing them to be dated to the reign of King Suryavarman I is an addition carved on the piers of the windows of the west wing of the east entrance pavilion and is in no way connected with the construction, since it concerns the oath of fidelity the functionaries swore before their sovereign; the building has to be older than this. This second state included the erection of a stone gallery (fig. 43), the raising of the central foundation and a new central temple. But from this time the function of Phimeanakas changed. It was no longer the central temple of a town, but the chapel of the royal palace, and the town built around the Phnom Bakheng of Yasovarman was shifted to be closer to the central authority. It was probably Suryavarman I (r.AD 1002-1049) who decided on the construction of the Bapuon (which was only completed in the reign of his successor, Udayatityavarman II, AD 1049-1066, who attributed to himself the entire structure), to provide his subjects with a public temple since Phimeanakas had taken on a private function. In effect, from this reign on there was no king who did not make modifications to the royal chapel. But little remains of all this effort for, in AD 1177, the palace was set on fire and when Jayavarman VII, in AD 1181, returned to Angkor, he observed that 'the capital was in ashes'. He undertook its reconstruction, bringing in particular modifications to Phimeanakas by completely rebuilding the upper part of the central shrine. These works were completed about AD 1190. Numerous changes continued to be effected on the monument until Angkor was abandoned, but they were in wood and the only trace of them remaining lies in the holes made into which to insert upright posts.

---

[9] J.G. de Casparis, *Short inscriptions from Tjandi Plaosan*, Jakarta, Berita Dinas Purbakala, 1958.

[10] As N. Aubin clearly demonstrated in her unpublished 1977 thesis with the Nantes School of Architecture, *Le Phimeanakas, temple montagne à Angkor*.

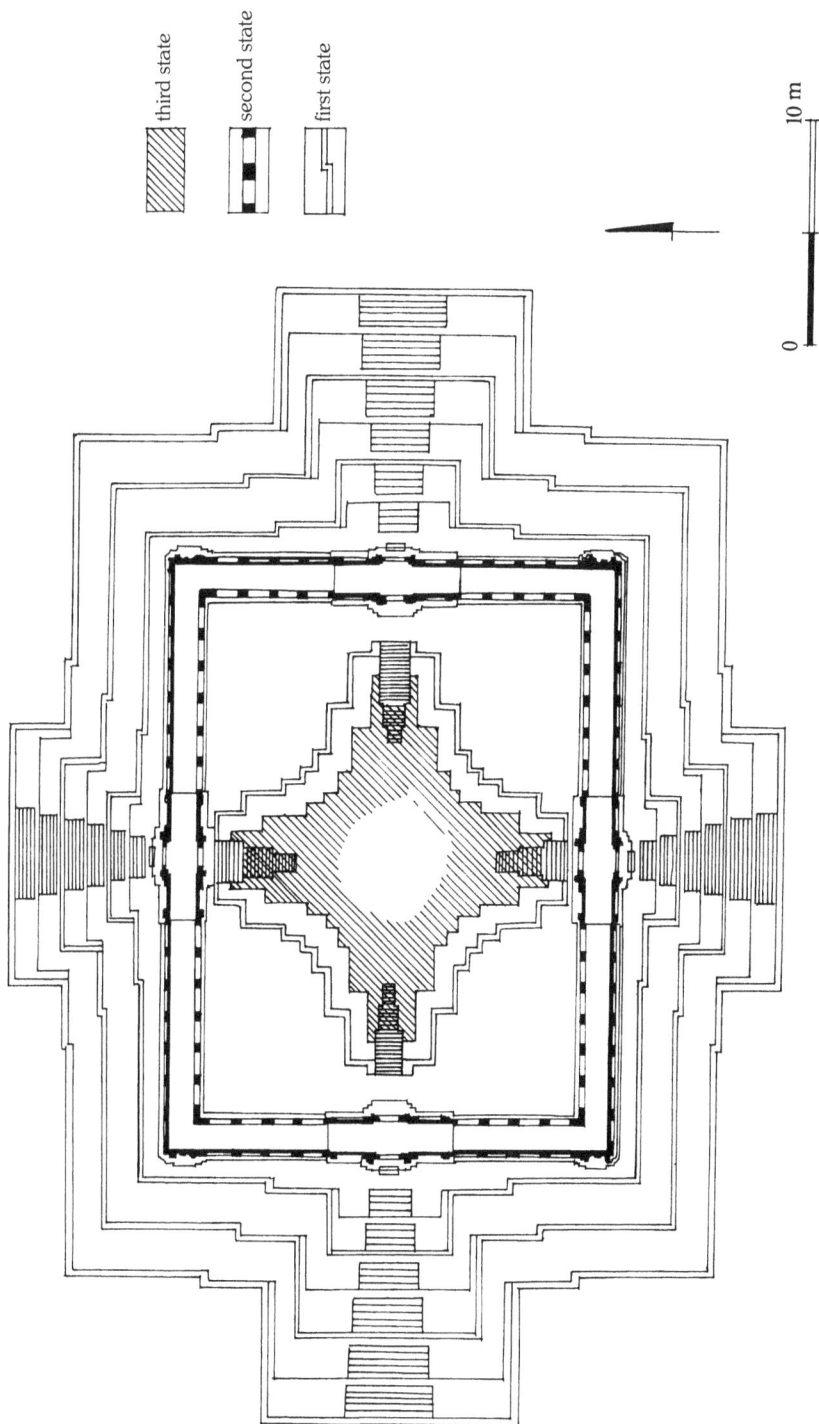

third state

second state

first state

0   10 m

43. *Different stages of construction of Phimeanakas, after N. Aubin.*

Numerous monuments at Angkor were modified by the superposition of
plans deriving from varied models. This is the case with the Bapuon, constructed
along the south wall of the enclosure of the royal palace. It is an important
building, some 100 m long on each side, and was conceived as a Shivaite
temple. After being used and maintained, with several modifications, it was
abandoned, probably during the fourteenth century, and then re-occupied
during the fifteenth century. Though its adherence to Hinduism, in spite of its
ruinous state, could not be doubted, it was transformed into a Buddhist shrine
with the construction, on the west face of the second storey, of a giant sleeping
Buddha, more than 60 m long (fig. 44), following a model which was to have
many copies, particularly in Thailand.

This was not the only monument at Angkor to be re-utilized in that period.
The Phnom Bakheng of Yasovarman, originally dedicated to Shiva, had its five
sanctuaries on the upper terrace partly or completely enveloped by the base
of a seated Buddha statue (fig. 45). This kind of change was not peculiar to
important structures; Prasat Prei, south-west of Angkor Wat, is a small temple
with a single tower which was originally Hindu and was changed to being a
Buddhist shrine in the sixteenth century. The shift from a Hindu temple to a
Buddhist shrine seems to have been an old tradition of the Buddhist master
builders. The incomplete Borobudur was covered with a Buddhist structure
which completely absorbs the earlier work and erased everything which could
indicate its previous appearance. The same is true in the Khmer kingdom,
though perhaps at first with greater subtlety; the temple of Bat Chum was
consecrated as a Buddhist shrine in AD 960, but its structure is that of a temple
dedicated to the Trimurti,[11] as if it was desired to smother the more widespread
religion and so express a feeling of superiority. Of course, when the Hindus
were dominant, they too broke statues and modified the reliefs, transforming
Lokesvara into Shiva and certain ascetics into linga, but with less intention of
changing everything.

When a master builder creates for the persons making use of his structure
an obligatory circuit through it, as at Borobudur with its galleries, this circuit requires a certain length of time to complete, and the master builder at
Borobudur varies this by adding recesses in the galleries, extending the time
pilgrims—or visitors—spend there; but the time taken can be cut short by taking the stairways (the ritual of circumambulation only requires one stairway
to the east, and one follows the reliefs from the left of the east stairway). All
this architectural exploitation of time spent in the galleries, and the building
as a whole, is high art.[12] This is particularly so with the Buddhist monuments
where the rite of circumambulation can be practised, which implies a certain
length of time for their construction. This is probably the origin of the drama-

---

[11] The inscriptions of Bat Chum, K 265 to K268, have been the subject of numerous publica-
tions; see G. Coedès, *Inscriptions du Cambodge*, Paris, EFEO, 8 vols, the last published
in 1966.

[12] See S. Gideon, *Space, Time and Architecture*, Cambridge, Mass., Harvard University
Press, 1971, fifth ed.

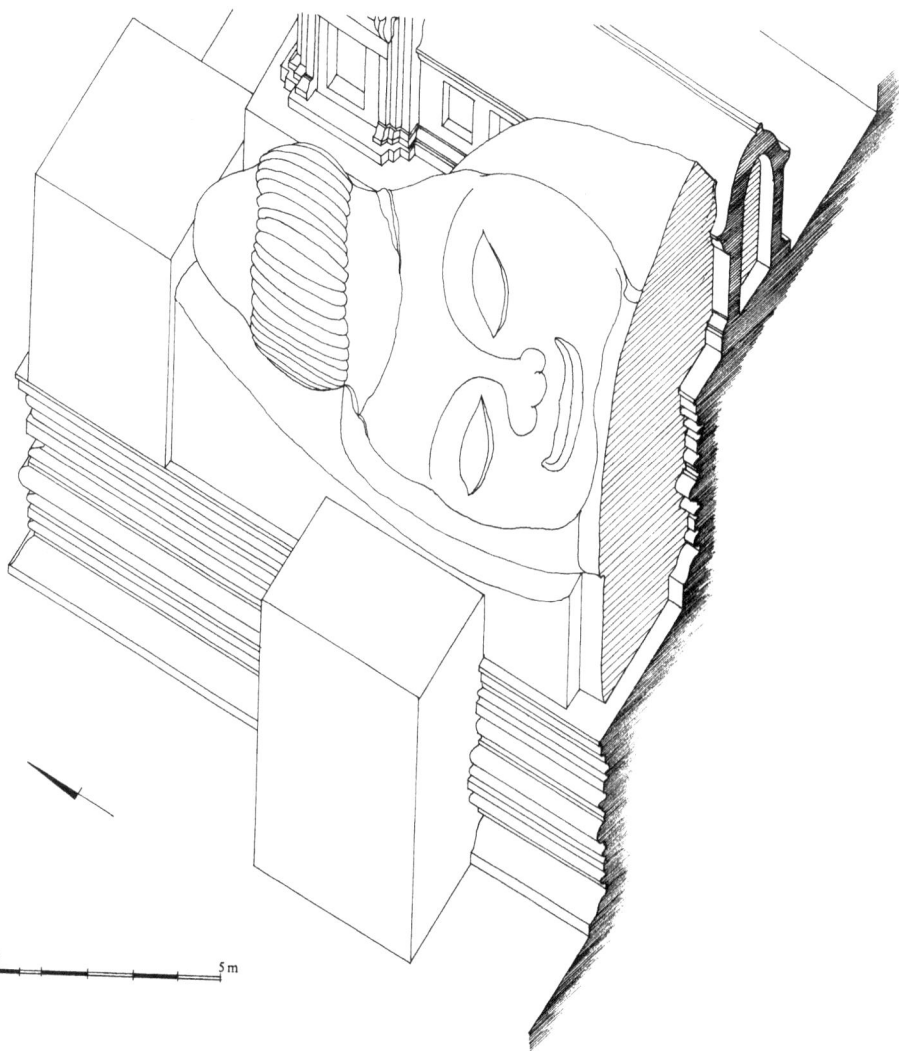

*44. Location of the sleeping Buddha, west façade of
the second level of Bapuon, Angkor.*

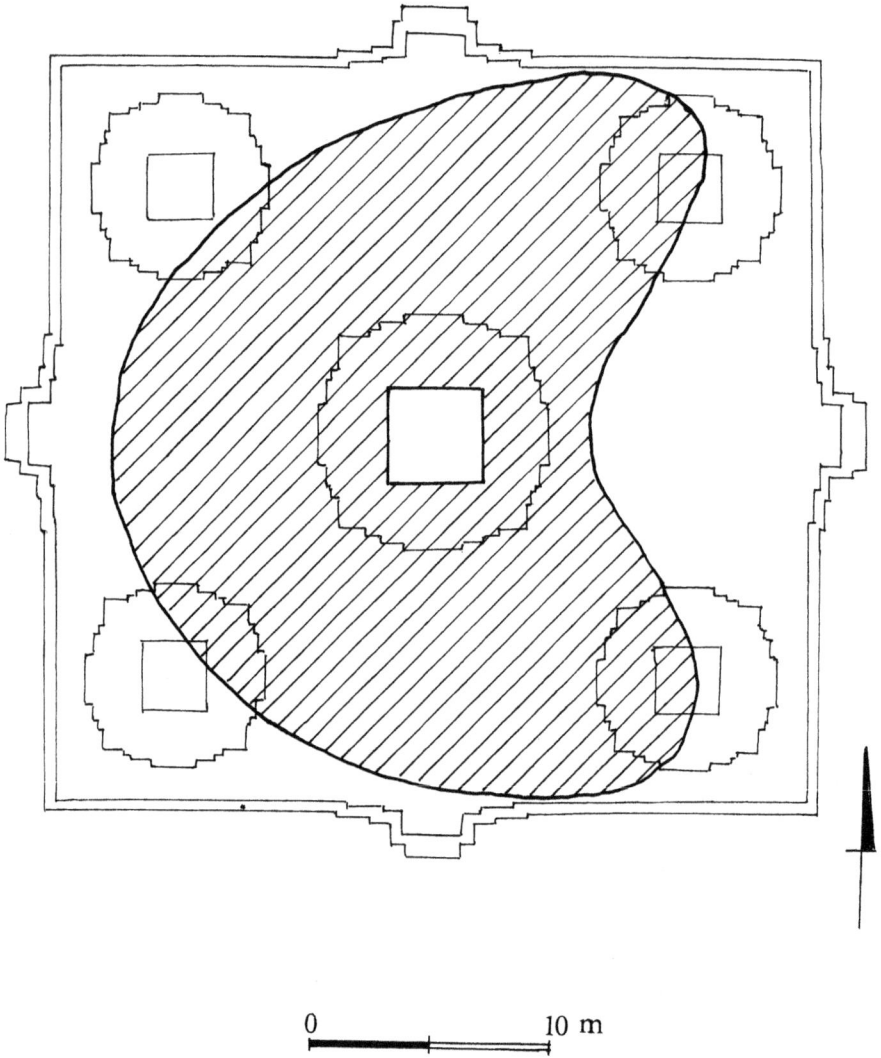

45. *Site of the seated Buddha on the upper terrace*
of Phnom Bakheng, Angkor.

tization of the structure, its completion being the conclusion of a programme, a drama, not only in space but etched in time. So when a king wishes to claim for himself the work of one of his predecessors (as Yasovarman did with Phnom Bakheng, begun by the preceding king, or Udayatityarvarman did in similar circumstances with the Bapuon), these additions are sometimes necessary for a technical reason and become the expression of this reappropriation. This is the case with Jayavarman VII when he had enclosed between two walls the access path to the Bapuon which is raised on short columns and was probably the work of Rajendravarman III. The structure was certainly in a very poor condition and some restoration was necessary, but it was also a way of taking over the Bapuon as his own, and of integrating it into the great undertaking of his reign, the laying out of the kingdom as a mandala.

The kings of Java and Cambodia used architecture, as did everyone else, to give a kind of order to the universe. There was a meaning in every detail of the construction. If the cells where the god dwell were dark, this was no mystery for the believers, the master builder and the person commissioning the building. In that space the king could without hesitation identify himself with the god and perhaps go further, placing episodes in his life alongside those of a divine hero, most often Rama, to whom the king compares himself. This appears in Java where, on the internal sides of the balustrades of the terraces at Candi Siva and Brahma in the ensemble at Prambanan (consecrated in AD 856), the reliefs illustrating the great Indian epic, the Ramayana, were carved in considerable detail. In a completely different style one can find the same cycle of illustrations at Penateran (consecrated in AD 1347) in east Java, on the reliefs of the foundation of the main temple. In Cambodia episodes from the Ramayana are very numerous among the reliefs decorating the Bapuon or Angkor Wat, to mention only the most famous examples. But it was King Jayavarman VII who without doubt wished to identify himself most with Rama. So on the huge reliefs which illustrate the life of the king at Banteay Chmar, the monkey Hanuman is shown on one of the panels of the south gallery (fig. 46) setting fire to the palace of Ravana in Lanka; this same episode is illustrated in the series at Prambanan and Penataran (fig. 47). The palace shown in Banteay Chmar[13] is very similar to that carved on the wall of the south external gallery of the Bayon. On this last temple, there is not such a clear reference

---

[13] This relief was described by H. Parmentier when the monument was first cleared, in an article 'Les bas-reliefs de Banteai Chmar', *BEFEO* X, 1910, 208. 'A. A tall person is seated in a palace surrounded by his court. A crouching man before him seems to present a report, indicating a lower picture which has disappeared; to the rear of the court numerous crouching servants bring presents or symbols of authority. A child comes down from a podium on which the servants have probably carried him, and some standing figures complete his retinue. C [sic]. The lower register shows a lightly-constructed palace, the triangular pediment is filled by a lion's head, the corners end in nagas. Under the gallery a small figure performs a war-like dance accompanied by music, before a group of spectators and guards. B. In the palace, between two scenes, an empty throne is shown; people bring rich vases, then in front of a closed door still others come with gifts; after them come persons who hurriedly close

46. Relief on the external south gallery at Banteay Chmar, Cambodia.

47. *Buildings shown on relief 169 of terrace A at Penataran, Java.*

to the epic, but B.P. Groslier demonstrated that the identification of the hero with Jayavarman VII was probably in the description of his life as shown in the Bayon.[14] The interest of this assimilation of the king to Rama, and his life to the development of the epic, is that one knows the end of the story, the happy ending and the triumphant return of Rama to Ayodia. One could say that this conclusion justifies all the treachery and all the suffering endured by his subjects, since in the end their happiness is assured if the country is transformed, according to a divine plan, into an ideal structure where the gods would be pleased to reside, into a mandala.

The liturgy of the mandala proposed to the believers a geometric schema marking out space in which symbols designating the gods were placed. A kind of theogony, a genealogy of the gods, is thus realized in which their relation to the centre, and the dependence of the gods on each other is expressed, but above all the relationship between the central divinity and the rest is made clear.[15] By transforming the kingdom into a giant mandala, with rectilinear roads and geographical spaces more or less rigorously marked out, the kingdom prepared to receive the gods in the spaces where they could reside, and the subjects of the kingdom could live alongside the gods, not immediately, but when all the roads were built, when the palace of the king, the central divinity of the system, was completed. Meanwhile one had to work with good grace in anticipation of the fabulous future.

The positioning of the mandala created by Jayavarman VII began from the moment he established himself in Angkor. But, taking account of the destruction caused by the war against the Cham, he was not immediately able to establish himself in the palace of his predecessors, so he ordered the construction of a provisional residence linked to a new reservoir (Neak Pean) with, in its centre, an ensemble of pools which were filled in the same way as the linga on the Western Baray but with more complex symbolism. The town associated with this new reservoir, Jayasri, was surrounded a wall marked with giant Garuda (the fabulous bird, the mount of Vishnu), brandishing snakes which they had overcome and on which they trampled (fig. 48). The gateways of the enclosure were preceded by gods and demons upholding the serpent which had served to churn the sea of milk around Mount Meru. This motif was taken up again for the construction of Angkor Thom, the permanent city which was entirely remodelled, chiefly in its central area. A new access was provided for Phimeanakas gaving the monument the appearance of a second Meru, the residence of the king made divine. But the real Meru, the public shrine, was the temple built in the centre of the town, the Bayon, which is not only an

---

the door behind them.' There is certainly some confusion in the numbering of the photographs used by Parmentier, but it can be seen that a part of what he describes has disappeared, like the tall person before whom Hanuman (as I think) is crouching has completely eroded.

[14] B.P. Groslier, *Les inscriptions du Bayon*, Chapter V, Les images de la vie du roi.

[15] G. Tucci, *Théorie et pratique du mandala*, Paris, Fayard, 1969, Chapter 4, La liturgie du mandala.

48. The garuda on the outer enclosing wall of Preah Khan at Angkor.

image of Mount Meru, but also an ideal representation of the kingdom. Mus showed that the gods and the place formed a unity, that is, the Bayon is not only a pantheon, but also an ideal geography of the kingdom, as are the Javanese temples of Candi Prambanan and Plaosan for example, as noted earlier. The geography shown in the Bayon is not only physical, as in the Javanese temples, but it is also historic; it was desired to express the future of the kingdom. During the fourth stage of construction, the passages linked the external gallery of the second level of the monument; the piers of the doorways to these passages, opening onto the gallery, carried inscriptions which indicated the gods present in the passages. These have been destroyed and the doorways which gave access to the gallery were walled up,[16] obliterating the inscriptions, which prevents the consideration of the epigraphic texts in their whole as forming part of the single unified ensemble.

G. Coedès and B. P. Groslier have already tried to separate the different texts into several categories: those carved before being placed in position in the décor and those which were carved at the same time or after in the place set aside for them. But these two scholars did not take into consideration the architectural history of the temple. The inscription in chamber E is mostly dedicated to the divinities at Roluos whose names are taken up again on the inscription in tower 27 (fig. 49), and can be interpreted in this manner: passage E, dedicated to the divinities at Roluos, was built at the conquest of the site and when this was truly incorporated into the kingdom, the passage was destroyed, and the inscription was taken to the tower of the second level located on the axis of the demolished passage. This evolution in epigraphy can be seen in another fashion: the spaces on the second level (38, 40, 41, 43, 44, 46, 47, and 49)[17] were transformed into chapels by topping them with a face-tower, at the end of the third stage of construction, so there are more or less contemporaneous with the passages. Several of these new chapels have a carved inscription which is, Groslier thought, added (with the exception of tower 43, but on the pier bearing the inscription, the décor was never carried out). It is only when chapels were needed to express the well-incorporated conquests of the kingdom that new face towers were erected and given new inscriptions.

The Bayon, for us, participates in the dramatization of the exercise of power as Jayavarman VII conceived it. The first stage of the construction expressed the kingdom in its great rigour, but in outline, as the king was not yet present at Angkor Thom. During the second stage, the king installed himself in the

---

[16] These doorways were filled with blocks of sandstone; the coherence of this infill is assured by the use of forcing wedges. This can be seen in the photographs illustrating H. Dufour and G. Carpeaux, *Le Bayon d'Angkor Thom*, Paris, 1910. These photographs were taken before the doorways were opened again. The forcing wedges can still be seen in some foundation layers still present from the sealing of the access doors to the gallery, passage E.

[17] For details concerning the architectural history of the Bayon; see B.P. Groslier and J. Dumarçay, *Le Bayon, histoire architecturale et inscriptions*, Paris, EFEO, 1973.

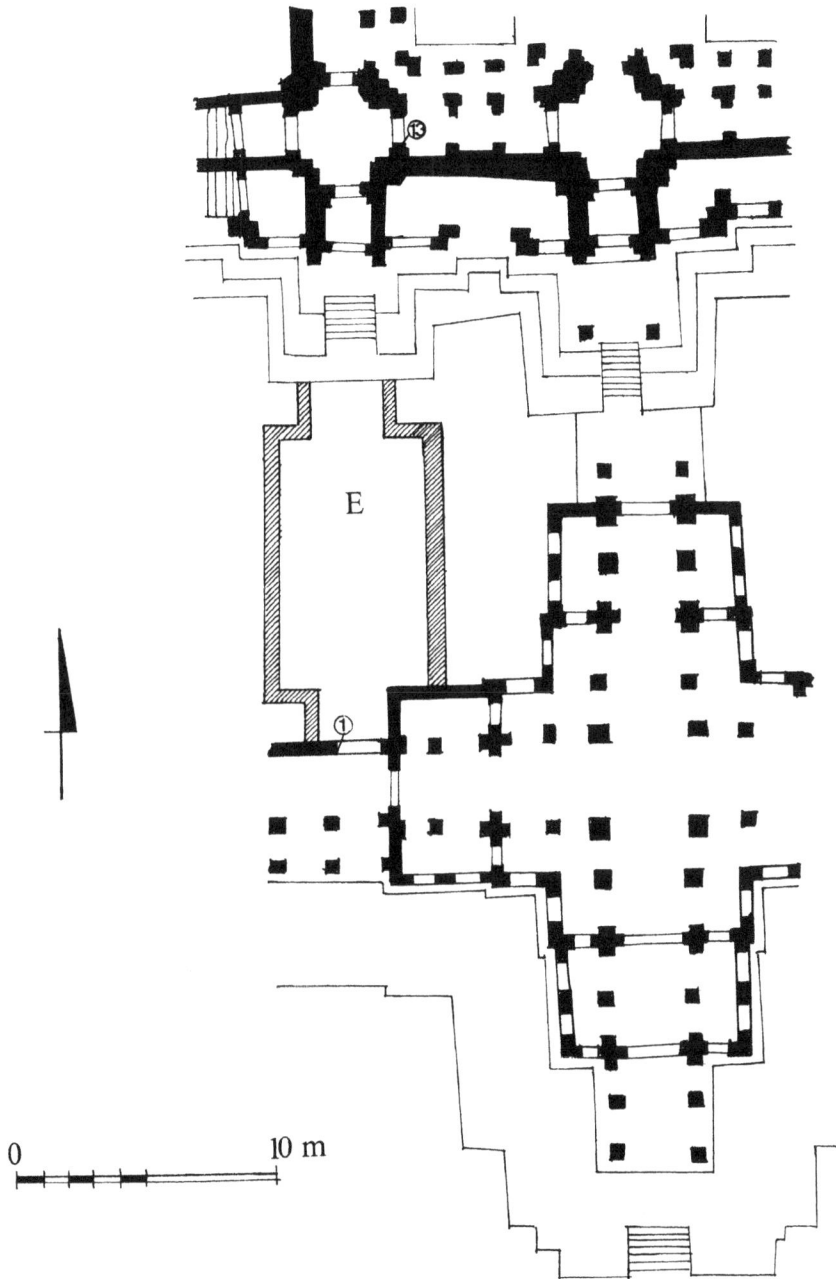

E

0   10 m

49. Plan of tower 27 and the passage-room E and the location of the inscriptions K 293 1 and K 293 13 at the Bayon, Angkor.

town and established his authority over the heart of the state. The third stage, where the central part of the monument shifts from a cruciform to a square plan, shows him squaring off his domain, and finally in the fourth stage shows the victorious king assimilating his conquests. This final stage has an element of theatricality since buildings were constructed only to be shortly after destroyed. The relationship with architecture in the reign of this king changed considerably; one did not build to shelter men or gods, but to participate in history, the history of conquests and their incorporation into the kingdom. So, when, out of necessity, the temple of Neak Pean (see Chapter II) had to be surrounded by a protective dyke against the rising waters of the baray, the occasion was seized to transform the temple, probably originally Shivaite, into a Buddhist shrine, containing a seated Buddha statue from whose navel came forth a jet of water. Architecture not only gave an order to the universe during Jayavarman VII's reign, but we are taking part in its temporal evolution towards its outcome, the creation of Ayodia, the ideal capital of Rama.

A conception of architecture as complicated as one intended to say everything could not survive its patron or its master builder, and Jayavarman VII's successors retreated to conventional architectural programmes which were altogether less ambitious.

IV

THE ARCHITECTURAL MODEL
AND COLLECTIVE INTELLIGENCE

When the model confronts difficulties in its laying out, it is modified so that it can be inserted in the new parameters, without, though, a new project being created. This is particularly clear with the Khmer tower-sanctuary, which was redesigned to take into account perspective effects; it was not a new form since the spectator was expected to reconstitute the original structure. The collective intelligence of the Khmers happily eliminated the bases of the false doorways and always reacted in the same way to this new parameter of composition by eliminating what could not be seen. Sometimes though, as at Ta Keo, the model reappears in an incongruous manner, with carved bases on the false storeys of the entrance pavilions which could not be seen. While architectural invention was evident over a long period, in the thirteenth century the original form, with the suppression of all that could not be seen, was used at Wat Banon near Battambang.[1] It is likely that, over a long period, architectural invention remained the prerogative of a few master builders, and the use of the model persisted for a long time.

At the beginning of the thirteenth century, arising from the dramatization of architectural composition, the angles of the temples with a cruciform plan were blocked, as had been done at the Bayon. This was also undertaken on several shrines outside Angkor, as at Prasat Stung, near Preah Khan of Kompong Svay. On this small structure, the blocking of the angles was limited to the central shrine (fig. 50) when it was not yet complete; in particular the redressing had not yet begun on the main structure. The blocking of the angles at Prasat Stung is not a squaring off of the plan, but a simple addition parallel to the initial plan, forming a small surrounding gallery. When a monument was begun after the decision to block the angles, the new form was incorporated into the project. This was the case with the central shrine of Wat Banon, (fig. 51). Here one can see how the collective intelligence manifested itself in the case of an existing structure which had just been built, when a change in its form was decided upon, but where the arrangement of the initial plan had to be taken into account. So the blocking did not occur on the shrine proper but on its projections. At Wat Banon, though, the blocking occurred on the main building since the construction was new, which gave the shrine an unusual plan, where the north-south axis is emphasized by the access to four spaces created in the transformation of the plan.

This incorporation of a new symbolism in architecture in Cambodia was done

---

[1] An elevation of the west façade of Wat Banon was published in *Documents topographiques...* op.cit., pl.LXXXVIII, where this composition appears.

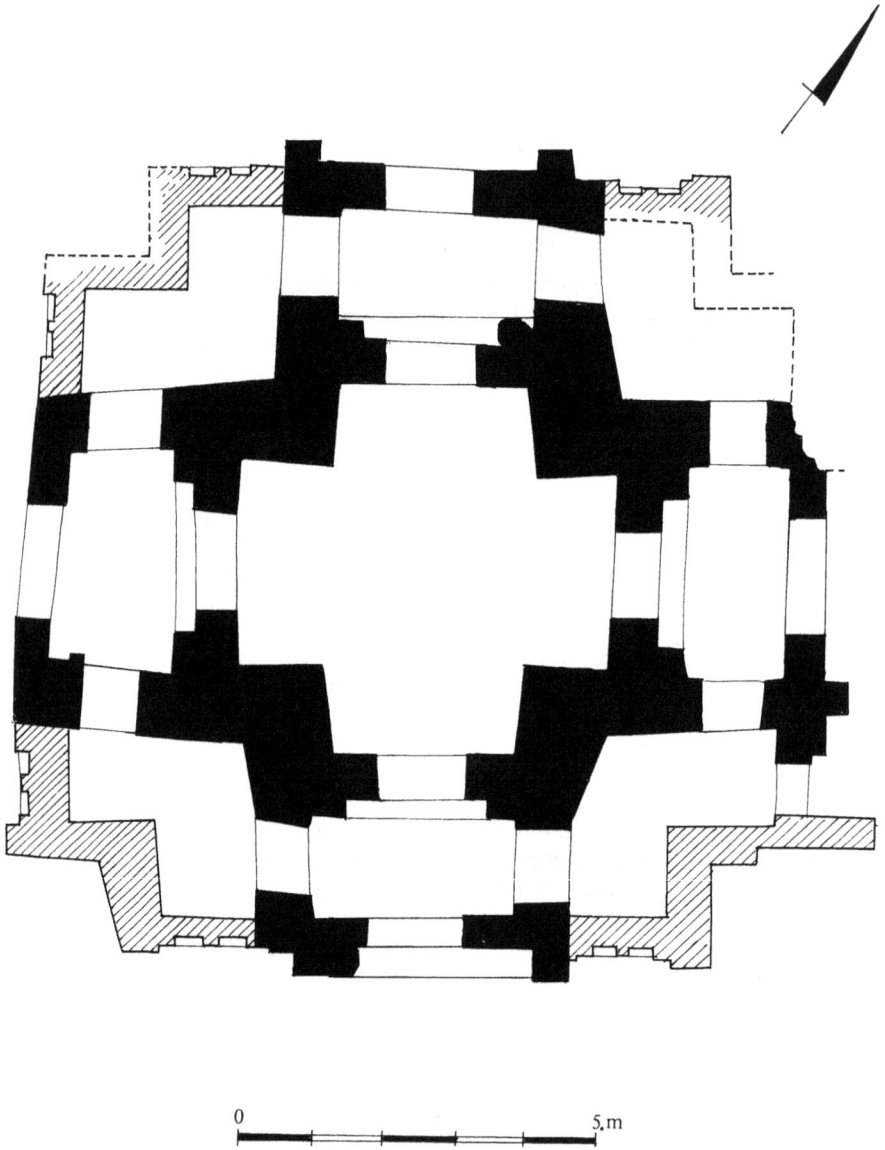

50. Plan of the central shrine at Prasat Stung (Preah Khan of Kompong Svay), Cambodia; the cross-hatching shows the added elements.

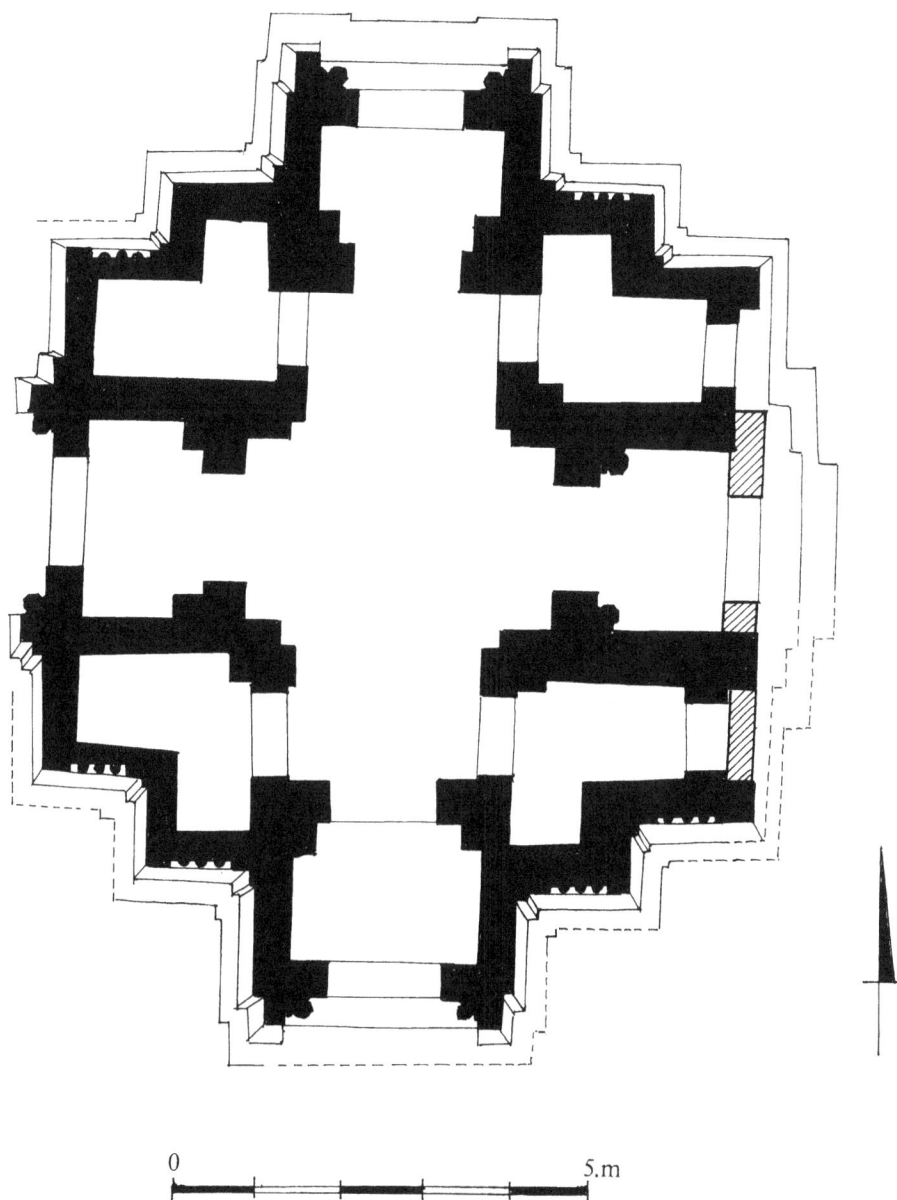

0   5.m

*51. Plan of the central shrine of Wat Banon, Cambodia,
the cross-hatching indicating added elements.*

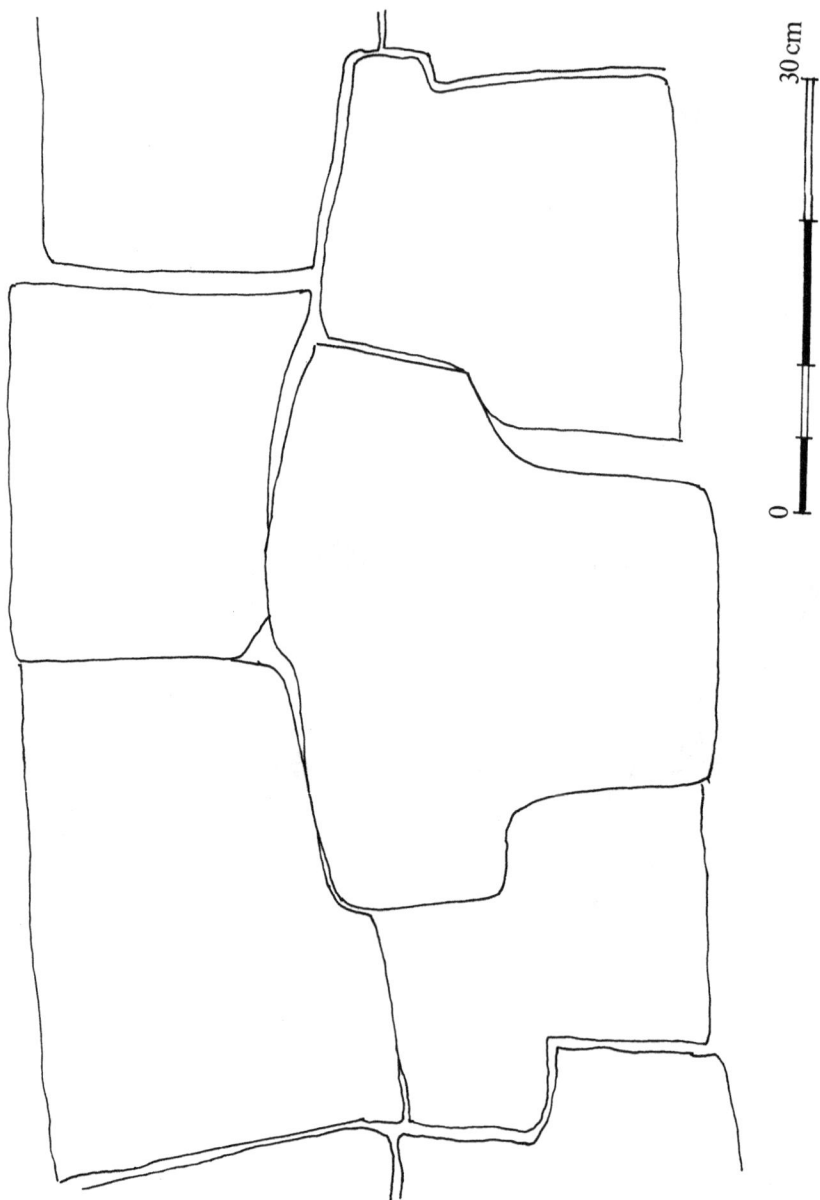

52. Crossette keystones in the gallery of the second level of the Bayon.

rapidly, separately from any technical evolution, and even when an invention as interesting as the crossette keystone (fig. 52) was used in a reworking of the Bayon, it led to no development. The doors and windows which had to be suppressed by the crossettes had forcing wedges giving coherence to the different layers, as had been done at the main worksite at the Bayon.

As noted earlier, changes in plan had been brought about at the end of the eighth century in central Java by modifications in the rites, where statues should no longer be visible from the outside and where ceremonies were restricted to the chief celebrant alone, enclosed in a cella which could only be locked from the inside. It was consequently necessary to modify the architecture in relation to these new parameters and to do so with structures which were sometimes very different and which did not lend themselves to this form. The adaptation to the monuments was made in accordance with the collective intelligence. On all the annex shrines at Candi Sewu, a door was inserted; the master builders were fully capable of putting in place the door frames, with many variations in techniques[2] but not in the general form of the ensemble, and while the additions were different according to the row in which they were found, the general layout of the building was respected. When this form had become the rule, it was incorporated into the new model; so the chapels of Candi Plaosan Kidul (the southern main shrine) were built with doors, door frames, and a portico, but the chapels surrounding Candi Plaosan Lor (the parallel northern main shrine) were built on a model without porticoes but with door frames and doors. This last form was perfectly in order and allowed the rites to be performed; the doors were indispensable. This was also true of Candi Lumbung, where the master builder did no more than insert door frames.[3]

It was probably at this period, the end of the eighth century, that the model of the sanctuary with a square plan in Java was taken to Cambodia and used there. However, an important difference (in spite of similarities) has often been observed between the Javanese and the Khmer towers. At Dieng and at Gedung Songo there are no false doorways, but niches; the monuments on these sites were mostly constructed before the changes in plan and the addition of door frames, before the ritual requiring the priest in charge to be enclosed.[4] In Java as in Cambodia, the doors of the cella can only be closed from inside; it was quite normal to show false doorways (fig. 53) rather than repeat what had been done at Candi Lumbung, close up the axial niches with wooden door frames.

---

[2] The different techniques of inserting door frames are indicated in *Candi Sewu…* op.cit., 22 and fig. 17. This great variety of techniques in insertion of door frames (for example, the eight main forms of sockets with numerous variants) probably shows us, as with Candi Plaosan which was built much later, that the donors were expected to undertake the changes, and this probably explains the language, Old Malay, used and the location of the inscription of AD 795.

[3] *Candi Sewu…* op.cit., pl.XXXI-IV.

[4] It seems likely that the Khmers never used the completely open sanctuary; even when a building has four entrances, as with Phnom Bakheng, the door frames were placed in the openings at the time of the construction.

20 cm
0

53 Fragment of the decoration on a false door of one of the secondary towers of the upper terrace on the Eastern Mebon.

When an important shrine was turned into a worksite, after the transformations of the original model became the rule, as at Candi Sajiwan,[5] the first model can be readily discerned, but the portico, though independent, is incorporated in the structure (it is embedded in the balustrade which surrounds the base of the structure), and the door frames are inserted in the entrance corridor. It can be seen to what extent the elements of the new model asserted themselves, but independently of a given form, and their arrangement is in some respects left to the interpretation of the master builder; this is probably one of the first manifestations of a composition independent of original models.

The Khmers inherited from India a form of roofing supported by curving beamwork, consisting of hoops; this was really an architectural form originally constructed in wood but which was on several occasions carved into the living rock, as with the Bima Ratha and the Ganesha Ratha of the seventh century at Mahabalipuram. The model of the structure for the Khmers was merely a form which they never apparently built in wood,[6] but they transferred this roofing into stone with a number of inconsistencies. At least from the seventh century, the Khmers covered their structures with so-called Roman tiles, which cannot be placed on curving beamwork. This though is what is shown in carvings, in considerable detail: carved in stone is a line of abutment tiles above the cornice and the edge bedding which supports the ridge finial. The representation of this type of roof covering over the galleries implies a perfect mastery of the technique of corbelling for the carver to have a sufficient volume of stone to illustrate the rhythm of the Roman tiles and the capping. After several attempts, in the twelfth century, this technique was perfected without, though, taking advantage of all its possibilities, not extending beyond a width of three metres, though in exceptional cases an arch of six metres was possible. For the construction of a larger building but with the same roof form, the collective intelligence of the Khmers transposed a technique used in wooden buildings: a roof covering of two slopes was placed on sagging beamwork so that it appeared to be a curved roof covering (fig. 54). This form was totally unadapted to the techniques used,[7] but its use was a reaction of Khmer collective intelligence. It was also used, in the same conditions, and the same lack of success, at Wat Phu (on the porticoes of the north and south palaces). The reaction was the same; this aberration was replaced by a roof covering of two slopes covered with Roman tiles, probably very soon after its construction.

It is doubtless with the simplest structures that the collective intelligence of a human group manifests itself. So we have seen that from an Indian origin, the structure of a wooden building is external. This was not just the case with

---

[5] *Candi Sewu...* op.cit., pl.XXXVI.

[6] However, in island South-East Asia the model was adopted and built in wood, and is still used today for granaries on the island of Lombok; the advantage of this construction is that it has a very large internal volume free of all roof supports.

[7] The technique consisted of having stones upheld by wooden beams inserted in the gables, and was used with some success at Bakong in Roluos, but for a roof covering with two slopes.

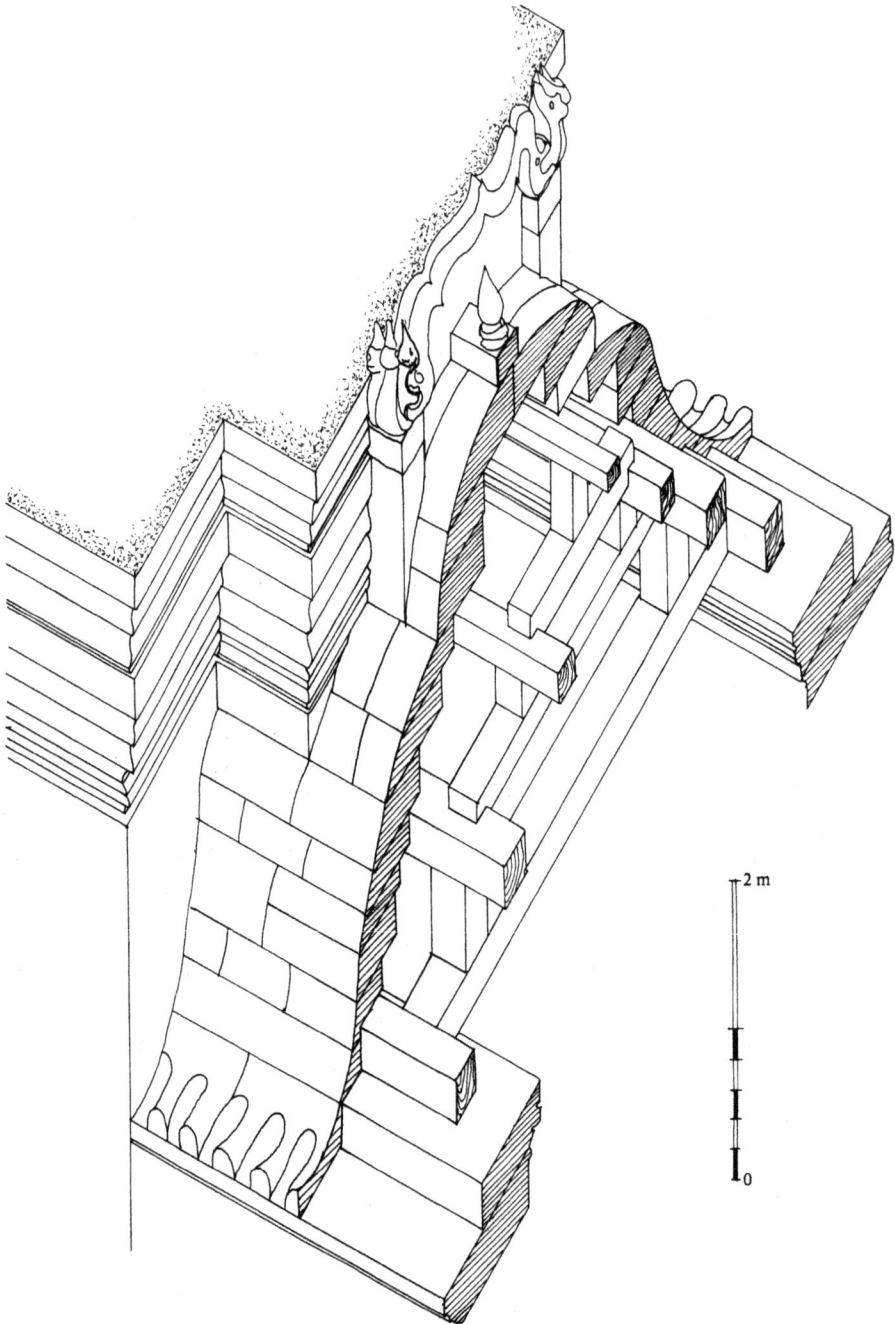

54. *Curving roofing on beamwork at the North Kleang, Angkor.*

religious architecture. For example, in Java, houses in the countryside have an external structure of panels, generally consisting of simple rush matting, applied to an internal front of load-bearing posts which remain visible. However, Javanese houses in the countryside gradually abandoned the use of wood, for many reasons, but the proportions of the original structures were retained, in particular (in the Kudus region), the internal eave gutters, which can only be justified by an oblong plan of the wooden roof beams which do not require a tie beam of great length, which could easily be avoided in a masonry building. When builders cover a rectangular structure with four roof slopes, they keep the same type of covering for two slopes, and the elements in the smaller sides are simply applied on the end of a roof piece (fig. 55). This last sign of collective intelligence has spread widely over insular South-East Asia since at least as early as the eleventh century, especially in Bali. On this island, probably around the fifteenth century, one of the elements adopted in the construction of a temple was the wantilan, a Javanese form called the pendopo, a huge pavilion with the roof in three parts. The form as adopted by the collective intelligence of the Balinese completed changely the technique. The Balinese carpenters felt they could not insert radiating beamwork (which indeed requires some skill) of those dimensions although this type of radiating beamwork is very common in Bali, even today, for structures with limited surfaces.

In a recent work, Nathalie Lancret[8] showed how the type of house known as umah, essentially rural, was adapted to the urban milieu. First of all, and this is at the origins of the conception, the space between the different elements of the house is reduced, and gradually elements foreign to the type are introduced: a garage, for example, which alters the original plan. But with the introduction of houses with one or more storeys, this new space had to be arranged and one can see the collective intelligence of the Balinese wishing to preserve, in structures which have nothing to do with the original forms, areas where the family rites can be observed and one finds one of the particularities of these houses is the clear differentiation between sacred areas and living space.

As has often been remarked, one only sees in perspective. Naturally this fact has been assimilated, and it can be clearly seen how the model of the Khmer prasat was transformed, counting on the memory of the spectator to restore the original form. These transformations have sometimes resulted in new forms which, in themselves, have been seen through perspective and are coherent only from certain viewing points when, because of the laying out, it is no longer possible to have an overall view of a structure and the eye can no longer reinstate the original image.[9] The collective intelligence transformed the model which was not understood to give it a new coherence. In the enclosure

---

[8] *La maison balinaise en secteur urbain*, Etude ethno-architecturale, Cahier d'Archipel 29, 1997; see in particular the third part, La transformation de la maison du type *Umah à Denpasar*.

[9] This is the case, today, of many visitors to the Javanese monuments, who, because of the ruinous state of the enclosure walls have an aberrant view of the structures, with incoherent perspectives which give an appearance of the form which was not intended.

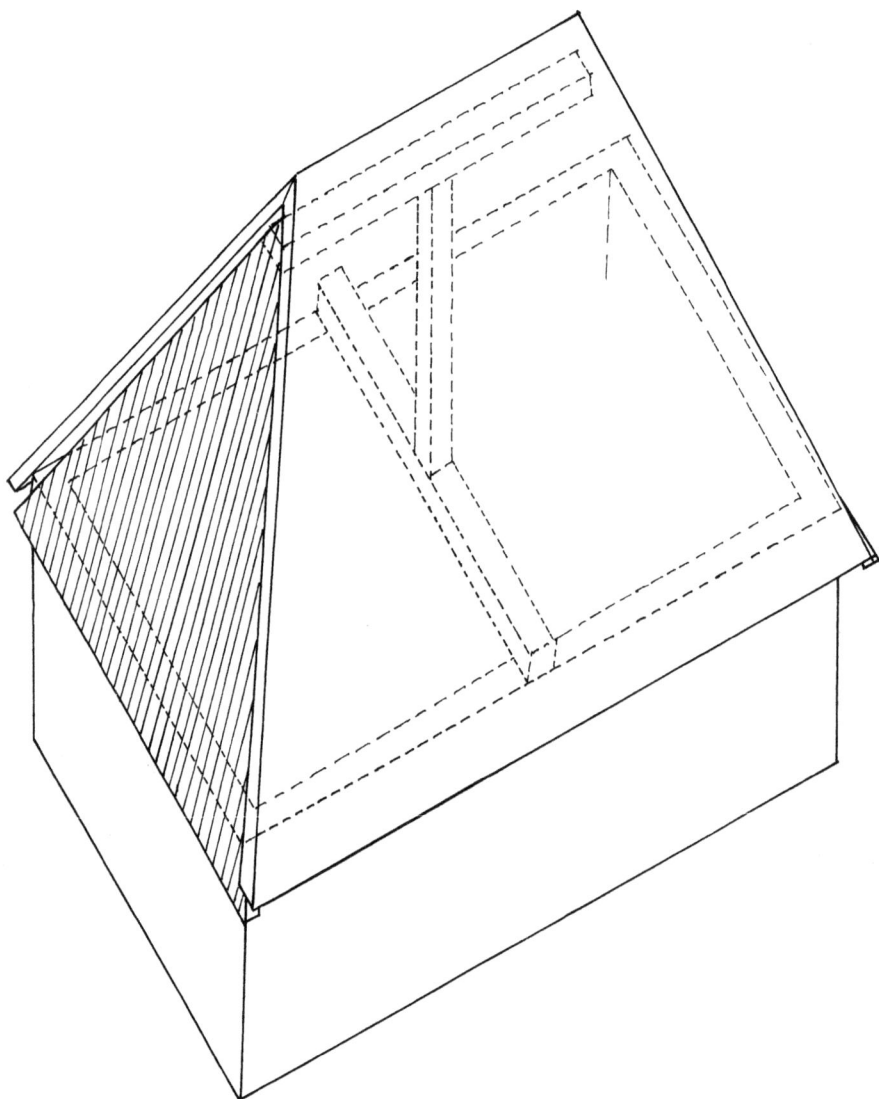

55. *Four sides of roofing on an oblong plan.*

at Prambanan, the three main temples conform to the same guidelines of buildings of the same type, from points of view located at the foot of the shrines
for the mounts of the three gods placed opposite the main sanctuaries. The
annexes known as the Candi Apit (fig. 56)[10] summarily reproduced the outline
of the main shrines, without there being a true anticipation of the completed
work (since for the most part it was the model that was reproduced). However,
the whole structure was conceived by eliminating some of the elements of the
model, so that the perspective could be seen independently from one viewing
point; this manifestation of collective intelligence is doubtless as the origin of
the model of the east Javanese shrines.

In Cambodia, the pyramids on which the temples were placed are constructed on the same model,[11] with perspective effects based on the reduction
of heights of the different tiers, with much concern for coherence as in Java,
but according to the volume of the shine at the summit, the collective intelligence adapted the model to the site. The pyramid of Baksei Chamkrong is
not different in its composition from those at Pre Rup or Ta Keo, except in
volume. Consequently the master builder transformed the proportions without
inventing a new form; in each case it is a pyramid with three storeys, with a
perspective effect to make it appear higher than reality. The master builder
knew that the structure, once completed, would please since it conformed to
pre-existing models.

When the modifications of the model, caused by collective intelligence,
constituted a new form whose links with acquired knowledge were apparent,
if the modified structure remained in place in the same environment, in the
same enclosure for the Candi Apit, its novelty only appeared much later, when
it became part of the acquired knowledge as an original independent form.[12]
When the master builders made use of it, as with the superposition of rows of
antefixes at the summit of the Candi Apit, it served as the point of departure
for an invention, in anticipation of a creation, of new structures at Candi Pari
and at Gunung Gansir (see Chapter VI).

---

[10] The Javanese, when they gave names to these structures in recent times, after the original name had been lost, were not in error since apit in Indonesian means 'compressed',
'squashed'.

[11] But with slight differences in plan, as at Phimeanakas and Koh Ker.

[12] It is also the new appearance of the monument, more constrained, which played a role in
the compositions of the thirteenth century, in the creation in Java of a new model whose
intermediary stages have disappeared.

56. *Elevation of the southern Candi Apit at Prambanan, central Java.*

V

THE COMPOSITION OF AN ENSEMBLE
FROM MODELS

Architecture in Asia, even when it is new, refers back to models which are sometimes extremely varied in order to produce an original composition. This is particularly apparent with the temple of Tak Keo, where each of the elements comes from the acquired knowledge of monuments of the master builder, but has been recomposed in accordance with the building programme imposed on him. The construction of this temple was interrupted because it was struck by lightning; this fact was recorded in an inscription,[1] which dealt more with the resumption of work: 'To K. J. Hemasrnga, he gave a sahsarayajna, offered finery for the idol and the dancers, offered a five-branched arrow [for the summit of the tower], and stringed musical instruments. When lightning struck the prasat, he caused an expiatory ceremony to be performed, and he began to complete the prasat by buying stones... and elephants.'[2] In spite of its brevity, this text gives a good indication of the construction conditions of a large ensemble. Ta Keo is huge—it measures 109 x 120 m at the base, and is only exceeded, in the volume of stone used, at Angkor by the Bapuon and Angkor Wat—and its composition was the occasion of one of the first manifestations of architectural invention. However, for each element in the ensemble, existing models were used, whether for the small edifices on the terraces or the towers at the summit (fig. 57). These shrines are built with an exceptionally good quality sandstone; the hardness of stone normally employed is 3.5, but that used in the towers is 5. This good quality was probably selected because it allowed for a very high polish which produced an aspect similar to vitrification; some statues made of this kind of sandstone take on a startling brilliance. We have compiled the list necessary for the purchase of the stones mentioned in the inscription;[3] it was necessary to order 400 m³ for each of the corner towers, used in different elements; 1,350 m³ for the central tower with, at the beginning, only a dozen stones of standard dimensions. From this detail it can be seen how the model was elaborated; the order for the stones was made in relation to the construction of the proposed structure. Though the quality selected could possibly have evoked the vitrification of the temple by the lightning strike, the cutting represented so many difficulties

---

[1] Inscription K 277 was carved on the north pier of the east doorway of the east entrance pavilion on the second enclosure, and was published by G. Coedès, *Inscriptions du Cambodge*, IV, 154-6.

[2] This follows G. Coedès' translation of the inscription, lines 29-31.

[3] J. Dumarçay, *Ta Keu, Etude architecturale du temple*, Paris, EFEO, 1971, Annex I, Calepin des pierres de la tour nord-est du troisième étage, 38-49.

57. *Elevation of the north-east tower on the upper terrace at Ta Keo, Angkor.*

that the work was not even started.[4] The model was present, but as soon as a change was introduced in its execution (here the quality of the sandstone), the collective intelligence showed itself incapable of overcoming the difficulties of the cutting on such a large scale. The master builder was unable to envisage the consequences of this change. The large architectural ensembles, in these conditions, could only be an assembling of proven models.

It was the laying out of the structures in relation to others which provided meaning to an ensemble, but this could not be accomplished without considerable technical difficulties. The instruments used to determine the positioning of structures were very simple; until the thirteenth century it was likely that the Khmers only knew the alidade. This is the only instrument of this type shown in the reliefs of the Bayon (those on the south gallery of the first storey, east wing). These difficulties become evident at Ta Keo: the crossing of the diagonals of the different terraces do not meet on the same axis (in fig. 58, A shows the crossing of the diagonals of the terrace of the first storey, B that of the second storey, and C the third). It is likely that this was combined with the desire to shift markedly, by some 40 cm, the axis of the central tower towards the north, and this shift is found in other monuments, at the Bapuon and at Angkor Wat, for example. At the last-mentioned temple the dissymmetry is important on the first storey because it is in two bays, but on the topmost storey, the monument has its four axes positioned symmetrically.[5]

One can also compare two monuments with different building programmes but constructed at the same period at Angkor: Pre Rup and the Eastern Mebon in its present state. When King Rajendravarman returned to Angkor from Koh Ker, he ordered the construction of two monuments; their purpose differs and so does the plan of the whole ensemble, but the elements employed, taken individually, do not differ. The towers of the quincunx of Pre Rup have the same model but are on a different scale from the Eastern Mebon;[6] the same is true for the annex structures which have, in both cases, a rectangular plan and beamwork roofing.

This search for architectural expression by the laying out of different models is particularly noticeable in Java. About AD 830 a new wave of Hindu influence brought not only new techniques but also new rituals, in particular for the laying out of buildings. The centre was to remain open, which caused dissmmetry in the ensembles and marked the points where this space was laid out, which

---

[4] Some elements, in particular the pilasters framing the doorways were reinserted with sandstone of a more common quality, but easier to carve.

[5] Such dissmmetry in Khmer structures can be observed but space was not determined by setting out boundary markers. In the thirteenth century, though, at Angkor, when Buddhist shrines were established, their area was fixed by boundary stones, as with the sema at Prah Pithu.

[6] For the plan of Pre Rup our thanks go to M. Glaize, *Les Monuments du groupe d'Angkor*, Paris, 1963, pl.XIX, and the plan of the Eastern Mebon is taken from J. Dumarçay, Documents graphiques de la Conservation d'Angkor, Paris, A. Maisonneuve, 1988, pl.XXIV.

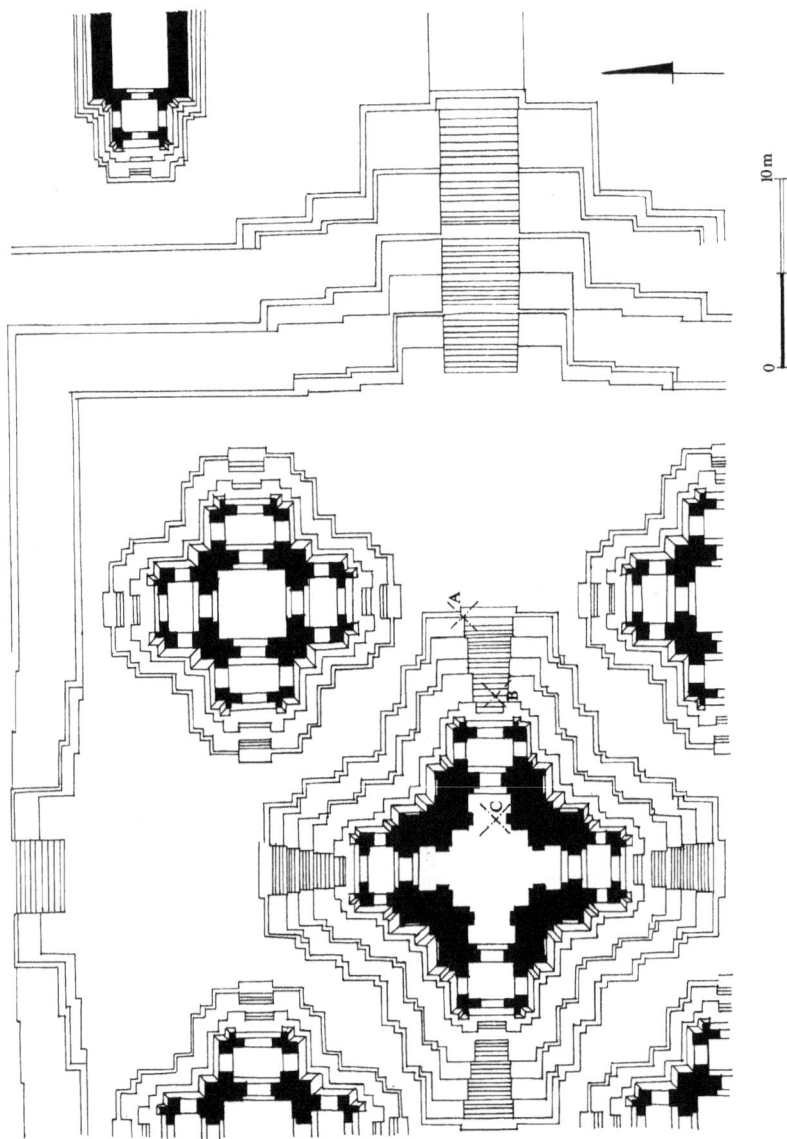

58. Part of a plan of the upper terrace of Ta Keo; (A) site of the crossing of the diagonals of the first enclosure, (B) crossing of the diagonals of the second enclosure, (C) crossing of the diagonals of the upper terrace.

10 m

0

would not otherwise have been easy to discover. At Prambanan (fig. 59),[7] the new points which marked out the area were placed on the ground itself, before anything else, and they were raised as the works progressed until the level of the upper terrace. The inscription dating the monument also indicates that the ensemble was constructed by important persons in the kingdom and that only the chief temple was commissioned by the king. Given the number of structures and their distribution in concentric rows (the few variations visible are internal, but taking into account the ruinous state of most of the small structures, we cannot be sure of this), recourse to models was essential if some unity to the huge complex was to be obtained. The construction of the temple also entailed a major irrigation project, the construction of a dam on the nearby Opak River. It was probably the destruction of this structure which to some degree explains the disappearance of the annex temples of the second enclosure on the west side. When the boundary markers served no further purpose, after the construction of the last buildings on the upper terrace, they were covered with a small shrine. This last ritual was rarely observed; most often the boundary markers were not preserved and a small linga was substituted if the temple were Hindu, as at Candi Sambisari.[8] Buddhist temples sometimes also had linga, as with Candi Idjo on the Ratu Boko plateau, or sometimes sema boundary stones.

The architectural history of each of the components of an ensemble and sometimes changes in interpretation given to a construction had important consequences for its plan. We have seen in Chapter III that Borobudur had numerous stages of construction and several successive meanings. This monument was placed on a very large site, the corners of which were marked by small temples;[9] only one has been discovered, that on the north-west corner, Candi Waringin Putih, placed on the alignment of the south-east/north-west diagonal of Borobudur. This monument was built to be dedicated to Hinduism, and the central image of the deity was a linga; it was probably built contemporaneously with the first state of Borobudur. When the main shrine was transformed into a Buddhist monument, the limits of the site remained the same. The site contained several other structures, Candi Pawon and Candi Mendut being the most famous, which were modified following the evolution of the main monument. These two temples were in their original state built of brick;[10] the base of Candi Mendut was covered with an andesite outline which married the old carved brick outline, and at Candi Pawon, the brick

---

[7]   The huge complex was probably consecrated in AD 856, as an inscription in Old Javanese indicates; this has been translated by J.G. de Casparis, Prasasti Indonesia II, Bandung, 1956, 280-330.

[8]   Candi Sambisari was built in the middle of the ninth century, close to a Buddhist temple which is now destroyed, whereas Candi Idjo probably dates from the end of the ninth century.

[9]   The limits of the town surrounding the temple of Prambanan were also marked at the corners and probably the axes by similar temples, without there being an enclosure proper.

[10] The temple of Bakong, at Roluos, in its first state owed a lot to the first state of Borobudur: a pyramid built in stone (in laterite, the sandstone facing coming later) surrounded by brick structures.

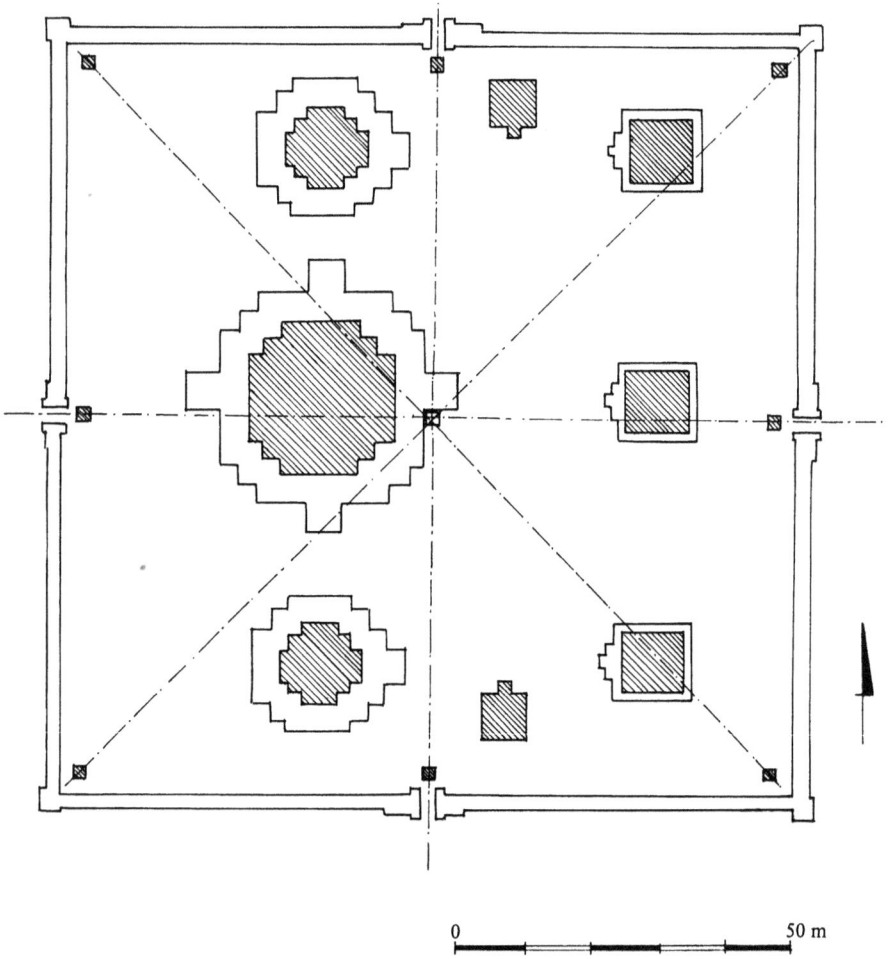

59. Location of the axes and diagonals on the upper terrace at Prambanan, Java.

base was entirely hidden by a new shrine. The site included not only religious structures but villages too; Professor Soekmono has excavated some of their most important buildings. The villages were centred on a small temple which was not necessarily Buddhist; the best preserved was a temple dedicated to the Trimurti, comprising three small towers, and we have seen that when Hinduism became the dominant religion again, a shrine, Candi Banon, was constructed close to Borobudur, within the old site.

The determination of a space is also, in its ritual, a way of indicating time; the nine more or less spherical stones[11] under the sema, the boundary markers in contemporary Buddhist temples, determine the sacred space of the future temple. They were placed on the ground around the temple on a small scaffolding, and a system of maintaining the stones in equilibrium above a small cavity below allowed them to fall into position at the same time. If a false manoeuvre resulted in one of the stones not falling at the same moment as the rest, the ceremony had to be repeated another day.[12]

It is in the framework of these different rituals that ensembles were constructed. Models had their own value, according to the desired meaning, and were applied to a scale corresponding to their hierarchy in the ensemble. The temple of Shiva in the Pramabanan complex is higher and bigger than the two dedicated to Brahma and Vishnu though these are built on the same model. This takes on a human value since it was probable that King Rakai Pitakan, who commissioned the structure, was in some degree identified with Shiva. This is particularly true of Candi Plaosan where the small shrines expressing locations are all identical, and it is the inscriptions they bear which fix them in the kingdom, not their form.[13] This is rather similar to the situation in the chapels at the Bayon; whatever their situation and the place they are supposed to represent, their plan and décor fit into the general structure, and this is true too of the different states of the monument.

When the person commissioning a sanctuary sought a more explicit expression of a mythical episode, as was the case with the construction of Candi Kidal (completed about AD 1260), where it was desired to show in architecture the churning of the sea of milk and several episodes of the Meru myth, the master builder, only having the models used at that period, placed them as best

---

[11] This evokes a ritual practised at Prambanan, where the successive boundary markers which served for the laying out disappeared, piled one on top of the other, under a small shrine. An excavation under the markers which surrounded the northern Prah Pithu at Angkor Thom, probably dating from the twelfth century, found no spherical stones. It is probable that the ritual involving them was a late one.

[12] Madelaine Giteau, *Bornage rituel des temples bouddhiques du Cambodge*, Paris, EFEO, 1969 studied in detail much of this ritual, though without considering this aspect of the ceremony.

[13] When the Indonesian government in modern times wished to show both the diversity and unity of the country in a single garden, the 'Taman Mini Indonesia', on the contrary the regional particularities of the architecture were selected to express each province. But it is likely that the original conception of this garden was not very different from the king who had the huge Prambanan complex constructed.

he could with a symbolic intention, whilst respecting the rituals of laying out. At first the space was determined by the nine usual positions,[14] then, when the structure of the future temple was decided, to suggest the sea of milk, the courtyard which was to surround the temple was built at a lower level than the surrounding soil; it could therefore easily be filled with water, suggesting the ocean surrounding Mount Meru. To ensure there was no ambiguity, the reliefs on the foundation base show a Garuda, the mount of Vishnu who presided over the churning, carrying Laksmi, the first person born of the churning, then this same Garuda presenting a container with the liquor of immortality obtained from the churning, and lastly a third relief shows the mythical bird holding a snake which served as a rope to perform the churning. The master builder only used elements which he knew, and placed them at unusual levels. There is no architectural anticipation, and the shrine is identical in its structure to other contemporary structures.

The variations are not only in the laying out but also in scale. We have seen that at Prambanan the hierarchy of the gods produced variations in height of the different buildings without the model being altered. An ensemble can, in its totality, be in conformity to the different types which it constitutes but can also be on a reduced scale. There is not only a hierarchy between the elements but also a reduction of the ensemble. This is the case at Banteay Srei (consecrated AD 967).[15] The three principal shrines conform to the usual model, with, though, important changes in the interpretation of the décor; because of the reduction of scale, the false doorways of the false storeys are shown whole, with door panels and catches complete. The perspective flight is only accelerated by the proportional reduction of the heights of the different storeys, but no elements are suppressed since, with the reduction in scale of the whole, everything could be seen and the mind had nothing to add to what was visible. It can be seen from this example how architecture was anticipated, but this was not done in a linear fashion, and there were several returns to the past. In a temple as complete as Banteay Srei, in spite of its date, the master builder, while respecting absolutely the model, did not wish his expression of it to appear absurd, and desired that the details of perspective effects remained coherent, in function with the scale of the structures (fig. 60) and also the possible viewing points of the spectator.

The composition of ensembles is probably at the origin of the appearance of true architects, from the abandoning of models, or at least their modification. When the master builder of Banteay Srei changes to a small degree the forms imposed in relation to what the spectator sees, he opens the way to the composition of Angkor Wat, where each of the elements is designed in relation to the whole, which is little more than an assembling of sometimes rather disparate models. The towers of the Eastern Mebon and the long building of its second enclosure reproduce, without variation, models, and are incorporated for better or for worse in the ensemble.

---

[14] Le savoir... op.cit., figs 14 and 15.

[15] A drawing of the monument was published in *Documents graphiques...* op.cit., pls XVIII-XXIII.

60. *Elevation of the south side tower of the first enclosure at Banteay Srei, Angkor, after a drawing of the EFEO.*

VI

ANTICIPATION OF THE COMPLETED WORK

The models created perspective effects which were utilized without truly mastering them. The suppression of elements did not transform the structure since the spectator was relied on to supply the forms omitted; there was no invention but a husbanding of resources. But it was from these observations, from this visual phenomenon, that the invention of the master builders began to be apparent, at first in a very modest way. Stairways were artificially enlarged, without changing the structure, but there was a real anticipation. When it was desired to embed the third level of the Bapuon in the framework which formed the second level, which implies a break from the model of Pre Rup and Ta Keo, the new form and the lower levels are similar in construction and position, but there is a desire to indicate an architectural break, as if the third level had an independent volume, as if the dwelling of the god was placed on the mountain, independently of it (fig. 61).

The first large monument where the master builder truly envisaged the result, independently of models, was Angkor Wat. The architect considerably renewed the forms while retaining his acquired knowledge of structures. This is particularly evident in the arrangement of the towers: the master builder made use of the old design in different false storeys, but these became invisible as they were hidden by antefixes placed on the edge of the cornice, which gives the structure a homogeneous line;[1] the divisions of the false storeys only remain in the memory. What is most striking in this new composition is the attitude of the architect to perspective. In the architectural models used up to then, a coherent form can only be established from certain viewing points; this was particularly evident in Javanese art of the ninth century, as at Prambanan. At Angkor Wat, the master builder did not seek to reproduce a model which would be coherent from some viewing point since everything assuring perspective disappeared behind the screen of the acroters, thus he produced a new form. It was necessary, for example, to foresee the terracing of the corbelling covering the stairways between the second and third levels, which was done very successfully. However, the great innovation of Angkor Wat was the new relationship foreseen between the spectator and the structure. The different screens formed by the enclosures allowed the architect to vary the viewing points and also required the visitor to see the monumental volumes from a different angle.

In Java, architectural invention appears later, in the fourteenth century, with the building of a great number of structures which break with the models of the thirteenth century. A desire to transform the structures according to the

---

[1] This was already the case at Banteay Srei (see fig.60), but the difference of scale created the transformations of this structure.

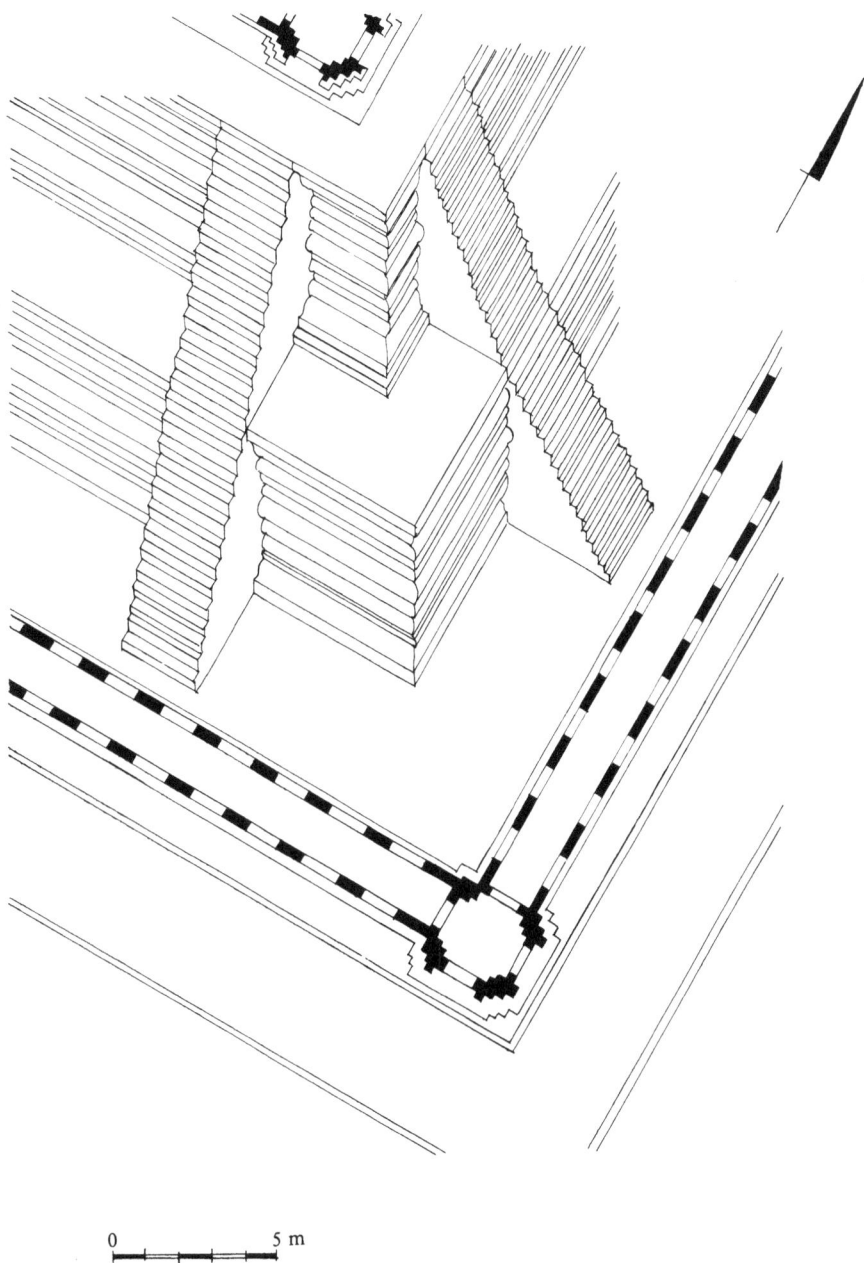

61. Axonometric drawing of the location of the third level, Bapuon, Angkor.

talent of the architect emerges. The proclamation of the charter of known as Sawardharma,[2] during the reign of King Kertanagara of Singosari, in AD 1269, freed the political authorities from maintaining the religious foundations which fell entirely under the control of the clergy: 'the domains of the clergy of all kind should be separated from the lands of the Royal servants'.[3] This surely allowed greater initiative to the master builders who, though remaining dependent on acquired architectural knowledge, created new forms. This is particularly evident in the brick constructions, like Gunung Gansir, Candi Jabung, and Candi Pari.[4]

At Candi Pari (fig. 62), dated to AD 1371 thanks to a dating configuration carved on the lintel of the entrance, and Gunung Gansir (fig. 63),[5] there is complete mastery of perspective. The movement of the relief of the mountain is shown on the finial of Candi Pari, by decreasing levels of antefixes, shifted in the relation to the centre (on fig. 62 the north-south axis is indicated by the letter A). This succession is interrupted by a landing supporting the miniature structures which are themselves images of the temple (this effect of mirroring structures in reduced size, common in architecture in South-East Asia, is rarely so well illustrated as in this monument). Above, the rows of antefixes are resumed to end in a landing with more reduced-size structures; unfortunately the structure is in ruins above this level and it is impossible to restore it.[6] At Gunung Gansir the same motif is used to suggest, at the top of the niches, the roof covering of a temple, and the master builder repeated the antefixes which decrease in size, and the reductions of the structure, but, so that there would be no ambiguity, birds are inserted in between them. This concern for scale in a structure was new in Java. The niche is indeed an image of a temple, but it keeps a modest position in the hierarchy of the structure; in spite of the reference to a real architectural construction, the composition is original.

This change in attitude of the master builders, who had become true creators, permitted a great renewal of architecture which was undoubtedly accompanied by new building programmes, or possibly a greater liberty in relation to them. The building programme of the temple of Angkor Wat is not easy to establish; for a long time there was an extended discussion as to whether the structure was

---

[2]   The charter of Sawardharma was studied by T. Pigeaud, *Java in the fourteenth century*, in particular in the volume of commentaries (IV, 381-390).

[3]   Pigeaud, op.cit., III 143-150.

[4]   Drawings of Candi Jabung and Candi Pari were published in *Le savoir*... op.cit., for Candi Jabung at pl.XXX-I and for Candi Pari at pl.XXXII-VI.

[5]   This monument is most often dated to the eleventh or twelfth century, because of a stylistic link with the monuments of central Java of the ninth century. We place it in the beginning of the fourteenth century. It is enough to compare figs 62 and 63 to notice the similar inspiration of the two monuments at the time when the master builders began to invent architecture no longer conforming to given models.

[6]   This perspective is coherent and it is possible to restore the point of departure in the composition of the perspective flight; see *Le savoir*... op.cit., 54, fig.40 which shows the point in the distance from where the motif becomes coherent .

*62. Detail in an axonometric drawing of the top of Candi Pari, Java;
the north-south axis is shown at A.*

63. Elevation of the upper part of one of niches in the main structure at Candi Gunung Gansir, Java.

a temple or a tomb.[7] The architecture had become completely independent of the building programme which it only expressed in a confused manner. Some elements in the composition seem to have no significance, other than to show the desire of the architect for a handsome structural development. This is the case, as we indicated above, of the link between the cruciform gallery with the terrace of the second storey at Angkor Wat, where there is some indication of a new influence, of Chinese palaces, or again, at the same temple, the corrections to avoid the unfortunate impressions of a hollow or recess which the set-backs of the outline produce (fig. 26).

In Java, the building programme is also diluted in the architectural forms whose meaning is sometimes precise, but their juxtaposition causes them to lose a clear meaning. Candi Jabung, built in AD 1354,[8] was destined to be a Buddhist shrine. The top of the temple forms a stupa, and other architectural elements are borrowed from the usual Hindu repertoire. In spite of the circular plan caused by the stupa, the main building is decorated on the axes with false doorways, with a capping rather unsuccessfully linked to the stupa, but this was an effort to create a structure independent of the acquired monumental knowledge of the period (fig.64).[9] This composition was assimilated by the master builder who supervised the construction of Candi Bahal I at Padang Lawas in central Sumatra, but instead of shifting directly to a circular plan, he placed an intermediary cruciform plan with the square cella. There was a true architectural renewal and an understanding of the problems which the shift from an orthogonal plan to a circular finial entailed, and the cruciform plan of the structure avoided empty spaces which would have appeared at the corners if the architect had simply retained the square plan.

A construction, no matter how original it appears, sometimes recalls disparate elements. This is the case with Candi Pari,[10] the originality of the composition of its finial we have just commented on, but the portico shows a gable of a building with sagging beamwork. This must have been a requirement of the building programme; the illustration of the roof must be there as a sign that the shrine was devoted to Vishnu (through the reference to granaries which, at that period, had, given their small dimensions, preserved sagging beamwork roofs and are frequently dedicated to Sri, one of Vishnu's wives). The master builder, faced with this requirement, reformulated the west façade of the building, so that suitable proportions were kept for the entrance; at the top the gable

---

[7] This formed a chapter in G. Coedès' book, *Pour mieux comprendre Angkor*, Paris, A. Maisonneuve, 1947, Chapter IV, Temples ou tombeaux. Prof. Soekmono studied in great detail the different meanings of the Javanese temple in his work *The Javanese Candi, function and meaning*, Leiden, Brill, 1995.

[8] The date is carved on the lintel probably at the time the monument was consecrated.

[9] Candi Jawi, dating from the end of the thirteenth century, has a circular capping which is also undoubtedly a stupa, but it seems to rest on the structure and has no link to it; the building comprises two independent structures placed on top of each other.

[10] Candi Pari is not the only structure to have this type of configuration; it can also be found in one of the porticoes of Belahan, see *Le savoir...* op.cit. pl.XVI.

64. Elevation showing the link between the upper part the doors and the uppermost stupa at Candi Jabung, Java.

engages the first row of antefixes and at the base, the stairway is inserted into the structure. This constraint was in contradiction of acquired monumental knowledge of the architect who had, though, integrated it into his work without it being ill-formed.

In India, when Catholic missionaries began to build their churches, their models were those of the period. They reproduced baroque churches on the spot in locally available materials and using local artisans. In Goa, where laterite was used, the carpenters, unaware of European techniques, adapted these structures which were new to them, using very ancient techniques in India which found their way to South-East Asia: the longitudinal beams are upheld by stone supports inserted into the wall. This is the same technique used by the Khmers in the eighth century, at Prasat Andet (fig. 11) and Sambor Prei Kuk (fig.16) to support the roofing. The use of these techniques transformed the initial model by eliminating the ceiling, and a new form was invented which led to the creation, largely individual, of an ecclesiastical architecture particular to this part of India. Later, at Pondicherry, when a cathedral was built, the inspiration was a French model of the seventeenth century. On the façade, one finds the accolades of the decorative repertoire so beloved of Clément Métezreau and Le Mercier, but there was true creation because the Indian master builder added to these splendid works which inspired him two disproportioned towers behind the façade (fig. 7), and this awkwardness is rather the mark of interpretations of these models, with a certain taste for inopportune additions and bombast.

Exceptionally the architect, having become aware of a form which seemed extraordinary to him or which required a tour de force, created an appropriate structure, not according to the requirements of a work programme, but those of a model which the use of the structure suggested to him. In 1796 in the town of Aizu Wakamantu in Japan[11] a tower was built for 'the easy progression of pilgrims'. This structure contained statues of Avalokitesvara representing the thirty-three temples of a pilgrimage in the west of Japan; the statues were regularly placed at the side of a double stairway (fig. 65) and allowed the pilgrims to perform their devotions without retracing their steps. The architect of this tower probably discovered a drawing of a double spiralled staircase in a copy which the painter Satake Shozan had made about 1785, and the original of which was recently discovered: this was the copy of plate 35[12] in the book

---

[11] These notes on the architecture of the tower of Aizu are mostly taken from an article of Kobayashi Bunji, 'The origin of "sazae-do" at Aizu (Ibaraki prefecture)—Baroque and the architecture of Edo,' *The Architectural Review* (in Japanese), vol.125, no.748, 1959, 341-343. This text was translated for me by Yamada Motohisa, to whom I am most grateful. The tower is today in ruins, but the restitutions of Kobayashi Bunji are remarkable.

[12] It is unlikely that the original drawing was by Leonardo da Vinci (who did not show a stairway but stair ramps, and who died in 1519, at which time the work on Chambord had only just begun) but was probably one of many drawings of the Chambord staircase, which is the case of fig.66, reproducing an anonymous drawing of the seventeenth century. It is very similar to the drawing reproduced by Joseph Mocson.

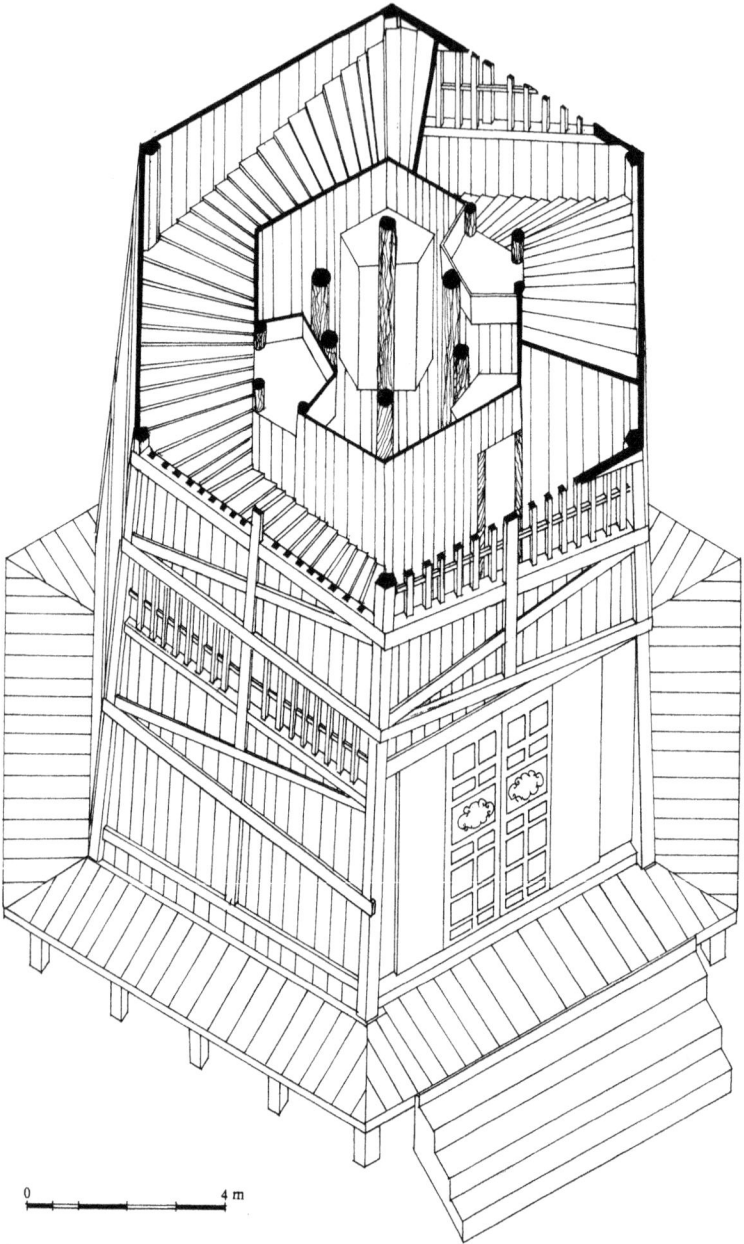

65. *Axonometric drawing of the stairway of the Aizu Wakamantu pagoda, Japan (see fig.4).*

of Joseph Mocson (1627-1700), The practice of linear perspective, published in London in 1670 but which only arrived in Japan after the lifting of the embargo on Western books, in 1722. The exceptional interest of this structure is that the architect, faced with an entirely new model, conceived an adaptation to a work programme which he invented for the occasion, which is a reversal of the usual process whereby the architect is confronted with a work programme for which he devises a structure (fig. 66).[13]

When Le Corbusier arrived in India, he had for a long time proclaimed his preference for a single trade on the worksite but, given the difficulties which Indian architects faced in constructing their projects in an acceptable fashion and, above all, the numerous small outfits operating on the site, his preference became a dogma. It was no longer the model of a structure which was to condition architecture but a technical doctrine. The impact of this selection was important and numerous structures are today built in Asia, for better or for worse, by a single trade. An Indian architect as talented as Raj Rewal[14] conceived his work, which he wished to link 'with the weft of Indian architecture woven in the past', by resorting in some degree to this principle. For example, the permanent exhibition centre in New Delhi, which covers 18,500 m², built in 1970-1972, was entirely constructed in reinforced concrete. Le Corbusier liked a certain rusticity in cement, but Raj Rewal added some finish which implies that the enterprises were given some training, but in spite of that, a building as ambitious as the Nehru Pavilion in New Delhi, with a surface of 2,025 m², demonstrates the brutality of cement. It is the good side of the influence of the dogma which was been taken up in very many cities in South-East Asia, but it also had an influence on the cost of buildings. The commissioners of structures, who often in South-East Asia build without an architect, construct without the aid of models, with a single trade, build odd structures which the inhabitants have sometimes been able to adapt to their expectations, but which are often indifferent architecturally and unlivable. In Denpasar, the chief town in Bali, many buildings are constructed without architects, on the model of Chinese shop-houses found in the cities of South-East Asia; they form a simple volume on a rectangular plan, open to the street (fig. 67), giving considerable homogeneity to the streets of towns in the region. In the nineteenth century, under European influence, elements of classical architecture were incorporated and gave to this real architectural model a form which supposed a certain number of artisans to build it, and led to all kinds of defects. So there has been a shift to construction with a single trade, the reinforced concrete entrepreneur. The width of the new form of shop houses is about 5 m, which preserves a kind of rhythm to the street, and has some reference to

---

[13] This figure, like fig.4, was taken from the drawings of Mr Kobayashi, whose work was presented to me by Mr Katagiri of the Nihun University of Tokyo, to whom my sincere thanks.

[14] See Raj Rewal, *Architecture climatique*, Electa Moniteur Monographies, Milan & Paris, 1986.

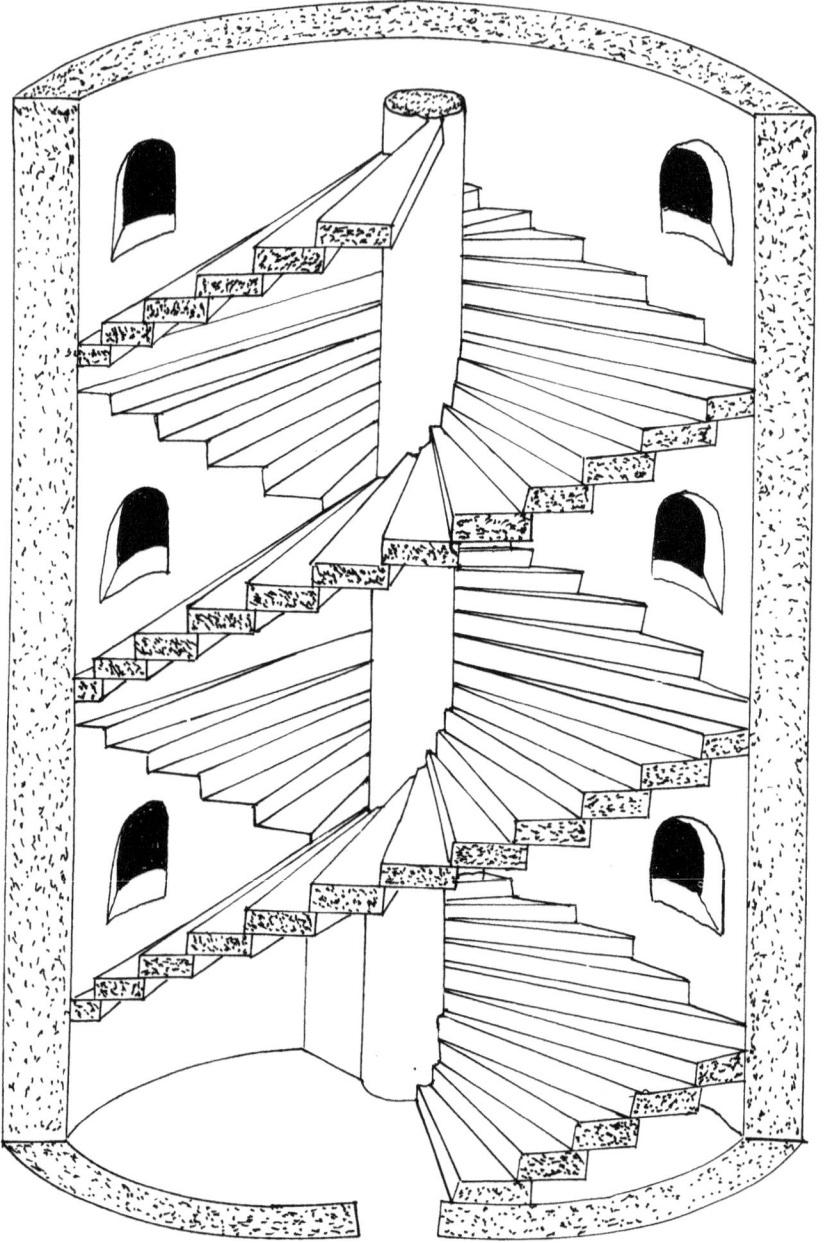

66. *Double stairway at the Château of Chambord, France, after a seventeenth century engraving.*

67. Present state of nineteenth century houses and divisions, Malacca, Malaysia.

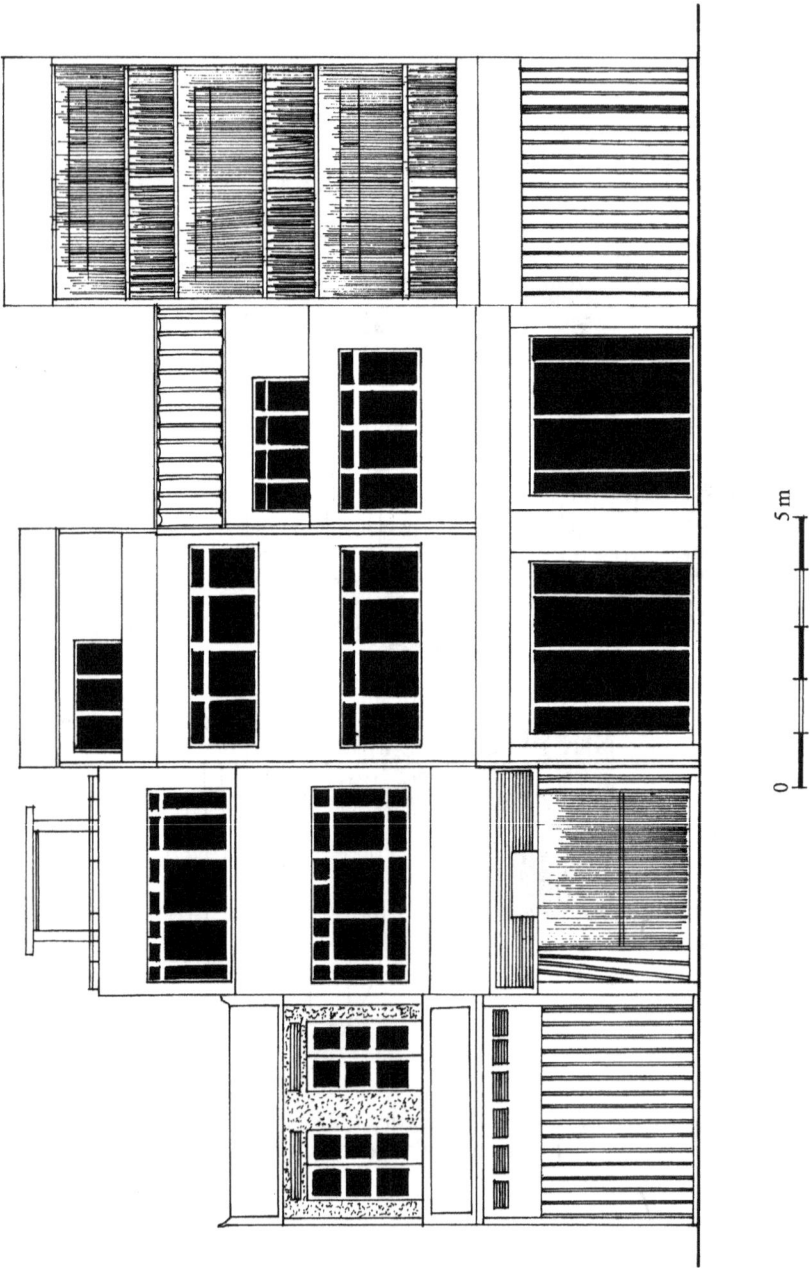

68. Reinforced concrete divisions at Denpasar, Bali, after a drawing by N. Lancret.

earlier designs, but there reference to the model stops (fig. 68[15]); it has lost all its coherence.

Architectural invention, in South-East Asia, can boast of magnificent successes, as with Angkor Wat in Cambodia, and Candi Pari in Java. These two examples have neither the same dimensions nor the same meaning, but their composition gave a new appearance to dramatic form, to the perspective vision of monuments. These two buildings, without breaking with the acquired knowledge of structures, show the individual invention of an architect who, turning to his advantage the constraints of his work programme and the techniques of the period, was able to create an original work. The work programme, in both cases, was to such a degree subject to the structure itself that is it difficult to re-establish it. The two master builders bore in mind one objective; they were building a dwelling for a god, and for that it had to be worthy of the divinity.

Architecture in South-East Asia has become ever more independent of the framework of the constraints of models, without, though, being able to free itself entirely from them. It is not difficult to find, in the smallest mosque built today in a Javanese village, the model of the great pendopo of the Majapahit civilization (fig. 69) or a model still older (fig. 70), shown on the reliefs of Candi Jago (built in the thirteenth century).

---

[15] This is taken from fig.25 of N. Lancret, *La maison balinaise* op. cit.

69. Folk art representation of a mosque in Yogyakarta, central Java.

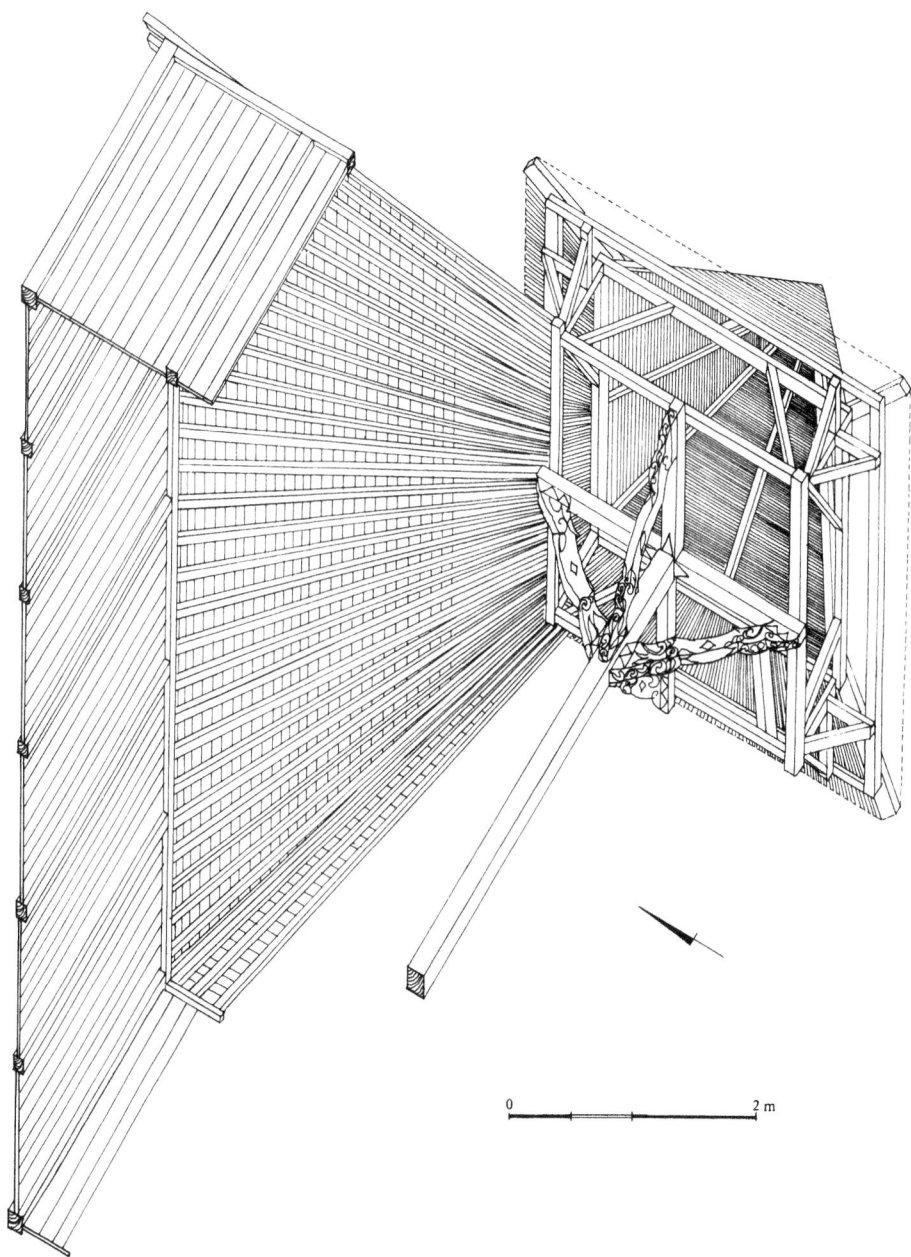

70. *Axonometric drawing of the mosque at Pekuncen, Java.*

CHRONOLOGY OF CITED MONUMENTS

All dates and periods listed are AD.

+/- 750	Candi Badut, first state (East Java)
End of 8th c.	Prasat Andet temple (Cambodia)
"	Octagonal towers of Sambor Prei Kuk (Cambo-dia)
"	Candi Sewu (Java)
"	Candi Lumbung (Java)
"	Kutisvara temple (Cambodia)
Beginning of 9th c.	Laying out of the Eastern Baray (Cambodia)
775-850	Borobudur temple (Java)
+/- 870	Candi Plaosan (Java)
851	Consecration of the last state of the Eastern Mebon temple (Cambodia)
Beginning of 10th c.	Ta Keo temple (Cambodia)
"	First state of Sras Srang (Cambodia)
"	Western Mebon temple (Cambodia)
967	Consecration of Banteay Srei temple (Cambodia)
+/- 1000-1060	Construction of the Bapuon temple (Cambodia)
+/- 1100	Thommanon temple (Cambodia)
"	Chau Say Tevoda temple (Cambodia)
"	Beng Melea temple (Cambodia)

1150 End of work at Angkor Wat (Cambodia)
1181 Construction work on the town of Angkor Thom
1185 Construction work on the Neak Pean baray (Cambodia)

End of 12th c.	Ta Prohm temple (Cambodia)
"	Banteau Kdei temple and the final state of
	Sras Srang (Cambodia)

+/- 1200	Ta Som temple (Cambodia)
"	Spean Prap Tos (Cambodia)
+/- 1250	Final state of Candi Badut (Java)
1260 Candi Kidal (Java)	

+/- 1347	Principal terrace of Penataran temple (Java)
1371 Candi Jabung (Java)	
+/- 1375	Candi Gunung Gansir (Java)

End of 15th c.- early 16th c. Spean Thmar (Cambodia)
1519 Beginning of construction of the Château de
Chambord (France)

1720 The Kew Pagoda (England)	
1775-1778	The Chanteloup Pagoda (France)
1796 The Aizu Wakamantu Pagoda (Japan)	
End of 18th c.	Pondicherry Cathedral (India)

+/- 1800	Nosa Chalderia church, Nanouar, Goa (India)
"	Chief mosque, Yogyakarta (Java)
+/- 1820	The Manora Pagoda (India)
+/- 1850	The Pekuncen mosque (Java)

INDEX

ABOUT THE AUTHOR

Jacques Dumarçay is an honorary member of the Ecole Française d'Extrême Orient, a specialist in South and South-East Asian architecture. He has taken part in the restoration of many monuments in Indonesia and Cambodia and is the author of several books and monographs.

His works in English include:

Borobudur, Kuala Lumpur, Oxford University Press, 1978
The Temples of Java, Kuala Lumpur, Oxford University Press, 1986
The House in South-East Asia, Singapore, Oxford University Press, 1987
The Palaces of South-East Asia, Singapore, Oxford University Press, 1991
(with Michael Smithies) *The Cultural Sites of Burma,* Thailand and Cambodia, Kuala Lumpur, Oxford University Press, 1995
(with Michael Smithies) *The Cultural Sites of Malaysia, Singapore, and Indonesia,* Kuala Lumpur, Oxford University Press, 1998
The Site of Angkor, Kuala Lumpur, Oxford University Press, 1998
(with Pascal Royère) *Cambodian Architecture: Eighth to Thirteenth Centuries,* Leiden, Brill, 2001

All these works were translated and edited by Michael Smithies, who also oversaw the English edition of the present volume.

www.ingramcontent.com/pod-product-compliance
Lightning Source LLC
Chambersburg PA
CBHW071820090426
42737CB00012B/2146